JIHĀD

The Islamic Doctrine of Permanent War

JIHĀD
THE ISLAMIC DOCTRINE OF PERMANENT WAR

Suhas Majumdar

VOICE OF INDIA
New Delhi

ISBN 978-81-85990-19-4

First published, 1994
First reprint, 2001
Second reprint, 2004
Third reprint, 2016

Published by Voice of India, 2/18 Ansari Road New Delhi.
Printed at Replika Press Pvt. Ltd.

Foreword

There was a time, not so long ago, when the exponents of *jihād* minced no words and pulled no punches. They were brutally frank in spelling out what *jihād* really meant.

But times have changed, particularly after the collapse of Christianity in the West and there rise of modern rationalism and humanism. Standards of moral judgment have increasingly tended to become universal, and no statement of faith can escape scrutiny simply because it is made in a book hailed as holy by some people. Defenders of *jihād* have been forced to develop an apologetics. They are now trying to protect by means of scholarship a doctrine which has so far been sustained by means of the sword.

In the present study, Professor Suhas Majumdar has seen through this "scholarship", and demolished it brick by brick. He has rescued the doctrine of *jihād* from under the mass of pretentious verbiage, and made it stand in its pristine purity. Let no one say any more that *jihād* does not mean what it has meant all along in the blood-soaked history of Islam, and what we are witnessing today in Kashmir.

At the end of it all, however, I wonder why scholarship should be needed for making people see what the ordinary common sense can see straight away. There is plenty of evidence that the common sense of the Pagans of Arabia had seen Islam for what it was worth when Muhammad proclaimed his prophethood. For common sense is after all a combination of natural reason and natural moral conscience which all human beings share in greater or lesser measure.

The story of why common sense had to keep quiet wherever

and whenever the prophetic creeds came to prevail (and among prophetic creeds I would certainly place Christianity as closest in tie and kindred to Islam) is yet to be pieced together. There is no better place than India for piecing together this story. For India's yogic spirituality has never worked counter to man's natural reason and natural moral conscience. On the contrary, yogic spirituality has raised that reason and that conscience to their highest stations.

A hoary and hallowed Hindu tradition recognises six types of gangsters. The śloka in which gangsterism stands defined, occurs frequently in the Itihāsa-Purāṇa and the Dharmaśāstras. It says:

agnidah gardaścaiva śastrapāṇirdhanāpahah
kṣetra-dāra-haraścaiva, ṣaḍētē ātatāyinah

(He who sets fire to (other people's properties), he who poisons (other people), he who wields weapons (for committing murders), he who robs (other people's) wealth, he who forcibly occupies (other people's) lands, and he who forcibly carries away (other people's) women—these six are gangsters.)

The same tradition prescribes a punishment for acts of gangsterism—the gangster should he killed as soon as he is sighted. The Gita, which deals with this subject among many others of high spiritual import, calls for this punishment when it says, "*jahi mā vyatiṣṭhā* (kill them, do not hesitate).

There is, however, another tradition which we meet in the Bible (at least in some of its books) and the Quran. This tradition has been elaborated endlessly and spelled out in unmistakable terms in the theologies of Christianity and Islam. In this tradition, the above-mentioned acts of gangsterism are supposed to have been sanctioned by no less an authority than Almighty God himself. And the person who perform these acts or advocate their performances, stand hallowed as apostles, prophets, saints, sufis, and the rest.

This tradition also prescribes a punishment. But not for those who practise or advocate gangsterism. On the contrary, it lays down that those who object to advocacy of gangsterism or resist gangster acts, should be put to death.

This second tradition arrived in India at first in the guise of Islam, and later on in the guise of Christianity, particularly in its Portuguese incarnation. Hindus were not slow to identify Islamic and Christian practices for what they were. The only point at which Hindus failed was to trace the Islamic and Christian behaviour patterns back to their systems of belief. It was a great failure indeed. For, in course of time, Hindus were led to believe, mostly by their own scholars, that Islamic and Christian behaviour patterns were not enshrined in the Bible and the Quran, and that Muslims and Christians could be brought round by appealing to them in the name of "true Islam" and "true Christianity". Mahatma Gandhi became the most eminent embodiment of this Hindu illusion, which has now become the stock-in-trade of one school of Secularism in this country—that of *sarva-dharma-samabhāva*.

Votaries of *sarva-dharma-samabhāva* are not likely to relish the charge that for all practical purposes they become passive accomplices of gangsterism when they equate Hinduism with Islam and Christianity, and advocate equal respect for the two predatory creeds. But that is the truth, and it has to be told in order to cure them of their smug self-reighteousness.

As for the second school of Secularism, namely, that which is rooted in Marxism and allied ideologies imported from the modern West, it does not pracitse *samabhāva* between Hinduism on the one hand and Islam and Christianity on the other. It is openly hostile to Hinduism, and stands unashamedly allied with Islam and Christianity. That is but natural, and this stance should be understood rather than assailed. For, in the ultimate analysis, Marxism, is that same as the other two creeds. All of them have their source in the Bible. Those who have applauded the gangsterism of Lenin, Stalin, and Mao, cannot be expected to thwart the other sort, particularly when it is aimed against Hindus whom they regard as the main enemy. They are bound to be active accomplices of Christian and Islamic gangsteriam.

New Delhi
15 July 1994

Sita Ram Goel

Contents

Preface

This is a slightly enlarged version of a small monograph I wrote in Bengali on the important Islamic subject of *Jihād fi Sabilillah* (war in the way of Allah). *Jihād* has five clear components, and a complete understanding of the subject requires a discussion of each one of them. Thus *jihād* stands for (1) Forcible expansion of Islam; (2) Destruction of infidels; (3) Establishment of *jizyah* on the subdued infidel population; (4) Plunder in the form of properties wrested from infidels; and (5) Plunder in the form of enslaved female and child population acquired from the vanquished infidels. In the Bengali monograph I discussed at length only the subject of plunder, which in Arabic is known as *ghanīmah*. I discussed and explained the other divisions from the text of the Koran alone, without illustrating them from the career of the Prophet. In this enlarged version I have devoted separate chapters to these divisions, highlighting the Prophet's activities in connection with each of them, and added some new appendices. It is my hope that, though increasing the size but slightly, I have left out nothing of real importance, and the theoretical aspects of this important Islamic doctrine have been treated here in full. I have not indeed described the numerous historical *jihād*s undertaken by Islamic zealots over the centuries; but I have discussed two of the *ghazwahs* (= *jihādic* campaigns) of the Prophet—his conquest of Mecca and his destruction of the Jewish clan of Kuraizah; these two form part and parcel of the theoretical apparatus of *jihād*. The Prophet's life and works form the bedrock of Islamic theology and are known as Sunnah. This, with Korainic sayings attributed to Allah and known by the Arabic title '*wahy*' (=revelation), are the final sources of Islam.

My ignorance of the Arabic language notwithstanding, I have tried to be as accurate as possible, and depended on the best translations of the Koran and the Hadis. The Koranic verses I have cited are mostly from Mohammed Marmaduke Pickthall's well known translation, but I have not failed to consult other reliable versions to ascertain Pickthall's faithfulness to the original. By all accounts, this faithfulness seems to be of a very high order, and though I have detected one or two small errors—not to mention his somewhat disconcerting affectation of an archaic English style—, I have on the whole stuck to his version even when alternative versions have seemed to render the meaning of the original clearer. This is because Pickthall was an Englishman who became a Mussalman by choice, and his rendering brings out his conscientious orthodoxy at every age of his version.

As regards the Hadis,[1] available English versions are by no means numerous. I have used the English version of the second most important collection, *Sahih Muslim*. This version is by Abdul Hamid Saddiqi, a Pakistani scholar. For cross-checking I have used a Bengali rendering of the important collection *Mishkāt-ul-Masabīh*. This rendering is by a Bangladeshi theologian, M. Aflatoon Kaisar. *Mishkāt* is a compendium of various canonical collections including *ahādīs* (= traditions) not reckoned canonical but recognised as important source materials to settle matters of dispute. On the whole, I have found that Abdul Hamid Siddiqi's version and that of Maulana Kaisar agree rather closely.

I have quoted rather generously from Sir William Muir's classic biography of the Prophet and also the painstaking work of Professor D.S. Margoliouth.

In India, critical studies of Islam are few and far between. Muslim scholars have done important work in translating the canonical literature, but they have shied away from critical stud-

[1] In the book I have uniformly used the capital letter when referring to the literature of the Prophet's traditions as distinguished from an individual tradition, *hadīs* (*pl. ahādīs*).

ies of Islam for obvious reasons. It is thanks to Shri Ram Swarup of Delhi giving a lead that Islam has started being studied in India in a critical manner in recent years. I could not use his pioneering study, *Understanding Islam through Hadis*, as this work has been banned by the Delhi Administration through a fiat which was aimed against nothing less than the freedom of scholarship itself. But without Shri Ram Swarup's guidance, I could not have started looking for the Hadis collections and the invaluable stock of information contained in them regarding the theory and practice of *jihād*. Warmest thanks are due to him, and I take this opportunity to acknowledge my indebtedness to him.

Sita Ram Goel's *The Calcutta Quran Petition* is a mine of information regarding the historical *jihād*s that took place in medieval India. His discussion of the theoretical aspects of *jihād* is not large in volume, but it has helped me in my research at every step as a sure guide.

Calcutta, **Suhas Majumdar**
June 20, 1994

REFERENCES

1. *The Meaning of the Glorious Koran*, by Mohammed Marmaduke Pickthall.
2. *Sahih Muslim*, 4 volumes, translated by Abdul Hamid Siddiqi.
3. *Mishkāt Sharīf* (in Bengali), Vol. 7, translated by M. Aflatoon Kaisar.
4. *The Life of Mahomet*, by Sir William Muir.
5. *Mohammed and the Rise of Islam*, by D.S. Margoliouth.
6. *Hidāyah* (the standard digest of Islamic tenets according to the School of Imam Hanifa), by Shaikh Burhanuddin Ali, translated by Charles Hamilton.
7. *The Calcutta Quran Petition*, by Sita Ram Goel
8. *History of Aurangzed*, Vol. III, by Jadunath Sarkar.

SOME IMPORTANT ARABIC WORDS

The best introduction to any Islamic topic is some familiarity with Arabic technical terms related to it, Islam has a large assortment of such technical terms for every aspect of its doctrinal structure, and the doctrine of *jihād* is no exception. Knowledge of some general terms is also necessary for a clear understanding of Islam.

General Islamic Terms

Wahy : Revelation with a capital R. Every verse of the Koran is wahy. The one and only source book of *wahy* is the Koran.

Sunnah : Literally 'practice', in Islamic parlance it means 'practice of the Prophet regarded as canonical and co-equal with injunctions proffered in the Koran'. The source book of Sunnah is the Hadis. It must be remembered that not every practice of the Prophet is Sunnah. His having nine wives at a time, for example, does not constitute Sunnah; but his practice of enslaving the children and wives of vanquished infidels is Sunnah par excellence. Again, the bloodless conquest of Mecca is not Sunnah, but the massacre of Banu Kuraizah is.

Sūrah : A chapter of the Koran.

Āyat : A verse of the Koran.

Hadīs : Literally 'a report', technically 'a report of some action or some saying of the Prophet regarded as Sunnah'.

Ahādīs : Plural of *hadīs*.

Sharīat : Generally, anything derived from the Koran and the Hadīs. In the restricted sense used in this book it refers to the literature of Islamic schools of jurisprudence.

Kāfir : An infidel, a non-Muslim against whom *jihād* is permanently established.

Mushrik : A non-monotheist Kāfir or an idolater, a term of strong vituperation in the Koran.

Munāfiq : A Muslim not wholly devoted to the cause of Islam or a renegade lukewarm in *jihād*, a term of full-throated abuse.

Kitābī or Ahl-ul-Kitāb : Jews and Christians whose scriptures (*Kitāb* in Arabic), *Taurāt* (Old Testament) and *Injīl* (New Testament), are recognised by the Koran as *wahy* (=revelation), but superseded by the Revelation in Arabic.

Terms Relating to *Jihād*

Jihād : Literally 'effort' or striving', doctrinally 'aggressive war for spreading Islam'. The full Koranic expression is *Jihād fi Sabilillah* (that is, *jihād* in the way of Allah).

Mujāhid : A soldier engaged in *jihād*.

Ghazwah : Jihadic war undertaken by the Prophet in person.

Ghāzī : Literally 'warrior', technically 'a victorious, infidel-slaying soldier of Islam'.

Shahīd : Literally 'witness', technically 'a martyr killed in *jihād*'.

Ghanīmah : Literally 'good fortune', technically 'plunder accruing from the successful conclusion of *jihād*. It has two parts: (1) Plunder of the vanquished infidels' property; (2) Plunder of the vanquished infidels' woman and children.

Ma Malakat ayman-u-kum : Literally 'that which your right

hand possesses', technically 'infidel prisoners captured in *jihād*, in particular captive infidel women sold into slavery and used for concubinage'.

Khums : Literally 'the holy one-fifth', technically 'the one-fifth of the jihadic plunder due to the Prophet or his latter-day representative'.

Fai : The whole plunder accruing to the Prophet (or his representative) when the infidel army surrenders without a fight. *Jizyah* is a species of *Fai*.

Jizyah : The poll-tax extorted from infidels vanquished in *jihād* but suffered to reside in their dwellings without loss of limb or life. The tax has to be paid in person and in a posture of abject humility. According to the *Hidāyah*, *Jizyah* literally means 'retribution money for obstinately clinging to one's ancestral religion'.

Kharājguzār: General expression for an infidel residing in an Islamic state indicating that he is a 'payer of the poll-tax'.

Zimmī: Literally 'a person under tutelage', technically it indicates the status of the *kharājguzār* in an Islamic state. The status is that of a resident non-citizen wearing out his life in a condition of semi-slavery.

Important *Ghazwahs* Mentioned in this Study

1. Raid of Nakhla (Late 623 AD)—The first blood shed in the cause of Islam.
2. Battle of Badr (624 AD)—The first full-fledged war against the Koresih of Mecca.
3. Expulsion of Banu Kainuka (624 AD)—The first Jewish tribe evicted from Medina.
4. Battle of Uhud (625 AD)—Defeat and setback for *mujāhids* under the Prophet by the Koreish of Mecca.
5. Expulsion of Banu Nazir (625 AD)—The second Jewish tribe expelled from Medina. The plunder of their properties was reckoned *Fai*.
6. *Jihād* against Banu Mustalik (626-627 AD)—The

Mustalik were an Arab tribe.

7. Battle of the Ditch (627 AD)—Also called Battle of Ahzāb in which the besieging Koreish were repulsed from Medina by the Prophets' superior generalship.
8. Destruction of Banu Kuaraizah (627 AD)—The third Jewish clan of Medina consigned to wholesale slaughter, their women and children being sold for buying horses and arms.
9. Expedition of Hudaibiyah (628 AD)—Presented as a pilgrimage because the Koreish did not permit the Prophet and his horde to enter Mecca.
10. Conquest of Khaibar (628 AD)—Surprise attack mounted on a non-Medinese Jewish tribe, which was reduced to the status of the first *kharājguzārs* in Islam.
11. Conquest of Mecca (630 AD)
12. The Battle of Hunain (630 AD)—A battle fought after the conquest of Mecca and followed by the siege of Taif.
13. The Tabuk campaign (630 AD)—The last *ghazwah* led by the Prophet.

Introduction

Jihād is one of the basic doctrines of Islam, but the average Indian's knowledge of it is both superficial and unsatisfactory. Hindus usually render the term as *dharmayuddha*, but this rendering is totally misleading. *Dharmayddha* means 'war fought according to rules laid down in the *Dharmaśāstras*' such as not attacking a person who does not have a weapon or has dropped it, not molesting an adversary who has surrendered, not pursuing a defeated enemy who has run away, not attacking the non-combatants in enemy camp, not harming the women and holy people and places in the enemy's territory, etc. Hindus have never known the concept of a religious or holy war, a concept which is characteristic of monotheistic creeds. Therefore, to the common Hindu, in particular to those who are ignorant of the history of the many religious wars waged by monotheistic creeds of Asia and Europe, *jihād* is a lofty conception. It is nothing less than war aimed at establishing what they consider righteousness in the world. Very few Hindus care to remember that the boy-emperor Akbar had become a *ghāzī* by slaughtering his helpless and fatally wounded prisoner Himu at the bidding of Bairam Khan in 1556 AD. Actually, even those Hindus who remember the story do not know the title *ghāzī* is conferred only on victorious, *kāfir*-slaughtering *mujāhids*.[1] In truth, *jihād* is war for the destruction of infidels (*kāfirs*) and infidelity (*kufr*). To obviate prevailing misconception, it is important to explain the meaning of *jihād* from the Koran, the Hadis and the corpus of theological works collectively going by the name of Shariat. As *jihād*

[1] *Mujāhid*—one who engages in *jihād*. Akbar's repudiation of the story of his becoming a *ghāzī*, without repudiating the title itself, is discussed in Appendix IV.

jihād is a basic doctrine of Islam and as its focus is on the *infidel*, it is not fit that Hindus should go on cherishing their deep-seated delusion regarding its meaning.

For the matter of that, even the average Muslim's knowledge of this doctrine is superficial. Every Islamic tenet is spread over the 6,000 and odd verses of the Koran in a desultory, haphazard manner. Few Muslims are competent enough to assemble the relevant verses enjoining *jihād* in order to get a systematic, coherent meaning. Such a work of systematization as the present one professes to be, could therefore be useful to Hindus and Muslims alike.

There is another, a more compelling, reason for present-day Indians to have a clear understanding of the doctrine of *jihād*. The so-called communal conflict in India which from day to day has been gaining in intensity has clear overtones of an all-out *jihād* that could burst upon us at any moment. This is not to deny that with the average Muslim the desire for peace and communal harmony is as strong as with most Hindus. But the common Muslim is mostly ignorant regarding how to channel his desire for peace without controverting the basic tenets of Islam. In the epilogue to this book, an attempt has been made in that direction. But it is not possible to take a stand against *jihād* without a clear knowledge of its meaning and its many-sided implications. This book is primarily a search for this meaning, and in this search our only guides are the Koran, the Hadis and the Shariat.

1

Jihād in the Koran

The Koran does not discuss a single Islamic tenet systematically and in conformity with the arrangement of its chapters. The combined body of Revelations from Allah which constitute the Holy Book of Islam appeared to the Prophet without any logical sequence during the 23 years of his prophetic career (609 to 632 AD), and this fact accounts for its haphazard arrangement. The Koran has 114 chapters and some six thousand verses. The verses of *jihād*, like those explaining any other doctrine, remain spread over a great, many chapters. This is the reason why, to an ordinary reader, the knowledge of any and every Islamic doctrine appears difficult, the doctrine of *jihād* being no exception.

A second and more important reason for the difficulty is that the Koranic verses do not deliver their full meaning without a knowledge of their relevance in the Prophet's career. The Koran is not the only source book of Islam, the so-called Hadis[1] collections share that role equally. In Arabic the plural of *hadīs* is *ahādīs*; these describe what the Prophet did or what he said. As a Muslim would put it, these narrate the Prophet's Sunnah (practice of the Prophet). In one sense, the importance of the Hadis literature in the life of a Muslim is even greater than that of the Koran. A Koranic text might admit of different meanings. Certainly different commentators could suggest different meanings of the same Koranic verse. But the relevant *hadīs*, in explaining

[1] Literally *hadīs* means a report. In Islam's technical vocabulary it stands for any report of the Prophet's actions or sayings as embodied in canonical collections also called the Hadis in a collective sense.

its meaning as exemplified in the Prophet's practice, renders the meaning unique for all time to come.[2]

Besides the Hadis, another source book for the Sunnah are the so-called *siyar* (plural of *sīrah*) or the biographies of the Prophet. These do not belong to the body of Islam's canonical literature but in so far as the events described in them are considered genuine by the ulema or the collectors of Hadis, these bring out the meaning of Koranic verses even more clearly than the Hadis. Thus the genuine biographies of the Prophet are important source books for Sunnah.

After these preliminary remarks the reader must understand that the literal meaning of *jihād* is 'effort' or 'striving'—a meaning, to all intents and purposes, unrelated to the sanguinary activities with which the word has become inextricably woven. The technical expression used in the Koran is *Jihād fi Sabilillah*, 'effort in the way of Allah'. But even this expression does not explicitly mention any sanguinary conflicts, and if we concentrate on meaning of words alone, we are likely to be led astray. When closely examined, the eight *sūrah* (chapter) of the Koran, the *Sūrah Anfāl*, and the ninth *sūrah* entitled *Taubah* are the truly jihadic *sūrahs*. But *jihād* is enjoined in many other chapters. Perhaps the most significant verse in this connection in Koran 8/39 which, in meaning, is almost identical with Koran 2/193.

These declare: "fight them until persecution is no more and religion is all for Allah."

In other words, Allah in 8/39 and 2/193 enjoins perpetual war for the destruction of the persecuting Koreish of Mecca, and by the same token, for the abolition of all non-Islamic religions the worlds over.[3] This according to the Koran is the best 'striving in the way of Allah'. This is *Jihād fi Sabilillah* in its most *comprehensive meaning.*

---

[2] Even *ahādīs* at times are found to be conflicting. We need not go into this.

[3] Cf. N.J. Dawood's rendering of the same verse, "Make war on them until idolatry is no more and Allah's religion reigns supreme", brings out the meaning more explicitly.

(2) Is this war allegorical? Since Mahatma Gandhi's allegorical explanation of the Kurukshetra war, it has been the fashion in India to consider all types of religious wars as wars, against the baser passions of the human mind. The contagion has not spared even Muslim scholars who are sometimes heard giving a non-violent interpretation of *jihād*. But such explanation is clearly contrary to Koranic verses. In the 74th verse of *Sūrah Nisā,* Allah says very clearly:

"Let those fight in the way of Allah who sell the life of this world for the other. Who so fighteth in the way of Allah, be he slain or victorious, on him we shall bestow a vast reward."

This verse clearly shows that there is nothing allegorical or metaphysical in the nature of wars that is *jihād*; it is armed war and nothing else. The idea has been further explained in another verse which says:

"Hast thou not seen unto whom it was said: Withhold your hands and establish worship and pay the poor-due? But when fighting was prescribed for them, behold! a party of them fear mankind even as they fear Allah or with greater fear, and say: Our Lord! why hast Thou ordained fighting for us? If only Thou wouldst give us respite for a while. I Say: The comfort of this world is scant; the Hereafter will be better for him that wardeth off evil" (K 4/77).

This verse describes the benefits of *jihād* to be enjoyed in the hereafter. Also it clearly shows that, instead of "withholding one's hand", *jihād* requires the waging of unremitting armed conflict. Obviously, this verse descended for the instruction of those Muslims who had been pleading against bloodshed and wanting "respite" from the duty of engaging in murderous confrontations. Historically too this verse is rather important. Before the Migration (to Medina) the number of Muslims (in Mecca) was not large, but even among that small number there were war-mongers whom Allah had to restrain as the issue of war in Mecca was dim. This comes out clearly in the first half of the verse. On the other hand, if the traditional date of the *surāh* to which the whole verse belongs be accepted, the second half of the verse shows that after the reverse at the Battle of Uhud (625 AD), the Muslim of Medina wanted to settle down to a peaceful existence. This second half was intended to rouse them to renewed warlike effort, and to revive their drooping spirits. Not only that. The verse seems to imply that a over and above the war-mongers there existed a body of Muslims who were essentially peace-living, and it required all the eloquence of Allah and his Prophet to rouse them and goad them into unflinching bloodshed. The lure of a felicitous hereafter was held up before them, and it was made clear that the abrogation of Meccan pacifism was final and irrevocable.

(3) The extent of violence and bloodshed permitted in *jihād* is also clearly stated in the Koran. The 5th verse of *Sūrah Taubah* makes no bones about the matter. Allah says in so many words:

"When the scared months have passed, slay the idolaters wherever ye find them, and take them, besiege them and prepare for them each ambush. But if they repent and establish worship and pay the poor-due, then leave their way free."

The meaning of this verse is clear enough. Profess Islam or else die"—such is the upshot of this verse expressed in the most transparent language possible.[4] But clearer even than this is the declaration embodied in the 67th verse of *Sūrah Anfāl*, which says. "It is not for any Prophet to have captive until he hath made slaughter in the land. Ye desire the lure of this world but Allah desireth (for you) the hereafter."

The historical background of this particular verse is important. Every student of Islamic history knows that the first landmark in the world-conquering mission of Islam was the Battle of Badr (624 AD). For the Koreishite idolaters of Mecca who fell into Muslim hands in that war, a proposal was mooted that all those captive be let off in lieu of adequate ransom. The idea was

[4] For the historical context of this verse see Chapter 10.

to earn some money by sparing the lives of the captured Koreish. Historians attribute this proposal to have originated from Abu Bakr. Another suggestion came from Umar who would have all the idolaters slaughtered. The Prophet accepted Abu Bakr's suggestion and, after killing a handful, let off the rest of the prisoners in lieu of some ransom money. Evidently this was not to the liking of Allah who would have a "slaughter in the land" rather than that his devotees should opt for "the lure of this world"—an expression which evidently stands for the ransom money accepted by the Prophet. As Mohammed Pickthall puts it, "The Prophet took the verse as a reproof, and they are generally understood to mean that no quarter ought to have been given in that first battle." The sanguinary nature of *jihād* comes out in this episode with the uttermost clarity.

(4) A variant of this ransom money was the famous *jizyah* or poll-tax or capitation-tax as it has been variously rendered.[5] The Revelation enjoininng the institution of this tax also occur in the Koran. *Sūrah Taubah* declares with thunderous clarity:

"Fight against such of those who have been given the Scriptures as believe not in Allah nor the last day, and forbid not that which Allah hath forbidden by His Messenger and follow not the religion of truth, until they pay the tribute (*jizya*) readily,[6] being brought low" (K 9/29).

This verse is of the greatest historical significance, and to explain it we must first of all know the meaning of the expression "those who have been given the Scripture". The Arabic original of the expression, *Ahl-ul-Kitāb*, and the Indian variant *Kitābī* as also the English phrase 'People of the Book', are also important.

In orthodox Islam the term *Kitābī* stands for Jews and Christian. This is because the Koran recognises the Jewish Scripture

---

[5] Literally it means 'retribution tax'—the retribution for obstinacy in refusing to renounce *kufr* (infidelity).

[6] For 'readily' most versions have 'with their own hands'. Actually in the law books the prescription is that *jizyah* has to be paid in person.

Taurāt (=Old Testament) and the Christian Gospels *Injīl* (=Evangel=New Testament) as Revelations equally authentic with the Koran but superseded, as this very verse indicates, only by the latter. The non-*Kithābīs* or non-Scriptuaries of the world are, in the Koran, designated as *mushrik* (=idolaters). With this explanation, the verse in question simply states that the lives of Scriptuaries may be spared in *jihād*, provided they pay the poll-tax "in humility and with their own hands". The verse is silent regarding idolaters; it does not specify if *their* lives too can be spared in lieu of *jizyah*. But as mentioned earlier, Islamic tenets do not derive from the Koran alone. There occur *ahādīs*—not recognised by all the schools of Islamic jurisprudence—which are supposed to mention the letting off by the Prophet of certain idolatrous (non-Arab) tribe in lieu of the poll-tax. The ulema, even to this day, are not unanimous whether Hindus deserve such immunity, even though the Sultans and Padishahs of Delhi had granted it by recognising their Hindu subjects as *kharājguzār* (=payer of the poll-tax) and *zimmī* (=held in tutelage). Even the fanatical Aurangzeb did not controvert this usage.

(5) Not only the poll-tax or ransom money. Another fruit of *jihād* is 'plunder' or 'spoils of *ghanīmah*' as the Koran puts it. The 69th verse of *Sūrah Anfāl* declares:

"Eat ye the spoils of war. They are lawful and pure."[7]

This injunction regarding "spoils of wars" will be taken up in detail in a subsequent chapter. For the present it will suffice to mention that this injunction is part of the group of injunctions laid down in the Koran on the subject of *jihād*.

To sum up, the following are the rules and instructions regarding *jihād* as laid down Koran:

(a) The *ultimate* object of *jihād* is to Islamize the whole of humanity. Since the Prophet's sojourn in Medina, this duty has

---

[7] This rendering is by Abdul Hamid Siddiqi, the translator of *Sahih Muslim*. Pickthall renders 'the spoils of war' as 'what you have won'. This seems to be wrong.

been permanently enjoined on Muslims over the length and breadth of the world.

(b) The *immediate* objects of *jihād* are four in number: (1) spread of Islam by war; (2) the destruction of infidels; (3) *jizyah*; and (4) plunder.[8]

(c) For *Scriptuaries* the imposition of *jizyah* is the rule, just as for *idolaters* the rule is mass-slaughter. But there are many exceptions to this general rule. Mass slaughter of Jew in *jihād* is eminently permissible, as the subsequent chapters will show. On the other hand, even idolaters can be let off on payment of the poll tax. The Koran has not published any rigorous rule regarding these matters.

(d) *Jihād* is by no means a war for self-defence. Historically the verse "kill the idolaters wherever you find them" (K 9/5) form an item in the 'immunity' granted to the Prophet in 631 AD regarding his obligations to the idolaters of Arabia. But as in every verse of the Koran, the implications of such immunity in respect of a particular set of infields embraced in due course idolaters of any and every country of the world. Such an injunction is necessarily informed with the spirit of extreme aggressiveness. For those who plead that the call of *jihād* is an injunction for self-defence, the so-called immunity verse of the 9th *sūrah* are the best refutation; but there are many other verses which confute the plea.

In conclusion it is only necessary to add that according to the Koran, the duty of *jihād* for any and every Muslim of the world preponderates over all other Islamic duties. This is brought out most clearly in verses 9/19-22, but these are by no means the only verses with a similar import.

In these verses Allah makes an estimate of the relative excellence of a Muslim who engages in *jihād* as contrasted with another who is engaged in pacific Islamic duties:

---

[8] 'Plunder' in *jihād* is actually twofold in nature. Plunder of property as well as enslavement of the female and child population of the vanquished infidels are both recognized as *ghanīmah*.

"Count ye the slaking of a pilgrim's thirst and tendence of the Inviolable Place of Worship (i.e. the Ka'ba) as (equal to the worth of him) who believeth in Allah and the Last Day, and striveth in the way of Allah (i.e. engages in *jihād*)? They are not equal in the sight of Allah... Those who believe and have left their homes and striven with their wealth and their lives in the way of Allah are of much greater worth in Allah's sight" (K 9/ 19-22)

The meaning of these verses is clear enough. The "greater worth' of the *mujāhid* "in the sight of Allah" necessarily renders him fit to obtain a greater reward here as well as hereafter. The reward here is an exclusive share in the spoils of war which is denied to the sedentary Muslim.[9] The reward hereafter is everlasting residence in the highest heaven which the Hadis literature designates as *Jannāt-ul firdaus*. It is to that literature that we must turn now to see how Allah's injunctions are confirmed and, in fact, added to in the Prophet's Sunnah.

[9] Vide also Koran 4/95 where sedentary Muslims are specifically mentioned and shrugged off.

2

Jihād in the Hadis

Before I discuss the contents of the Hadis literature, in so far as those pertain to *jihād*. I must tell the reader that only Sunni works of Hadis have been published in translation and even those translations are partial. The Koran is canonical scripture par excellence, and is common to all sections of Muslims. But the Hadis of the Sunnis is not the same as the Hadis of the Shias. Western scholars have studied most of the religions of the world, but even they have not cared to render the Hadis literature in English. The translations I have met are mostly due to the ulema of Pakistan and Bangladesh. It seems there is hesitancy even amongst the ulema in making the Hadis literature easily available to infidels. At any rate, their enthusiasm for making the Koran accessible to one and all is not matched by a similar effort towards popularising the Hadis literature. This is perfectly understandable if we consider the fact that the language used in the Hadis literature at times border on extreme coarseness and obscenity. It stands to reason that the ulema would not want to display this portion of their religious merchandise before the eyes of unsympathetic infidels.[1] But this very fact has rendered the work of scholarship difficult. One has to be not only a competent Arabist but has also to run the gauntlet of ulemaic apposition to secure authentic works of Hadis. The scholarly searcher has to beware of the bowdlerised and severely edited works of Hadis

[1] Cf Muir, "As to the Hadith, I altogether fail to understand how any translator can justify himself in rendering into English much that is contained in the sections on marriage, purification, divorce, and female slavery" (*The Life of Mahomet*, p. 334).

which would meet him at every step in his research. With this warning. I would lead the reader to a brief discussion of the Hadis literature of the Sunnis.

The *ahādīs* accepted by the Sunnis as canonical have been collected is as many as six works. These in Arabic are called *Sihah Sittah* which in plain English means the 'six authentics'. All these were considered canonical, but the collections by (1) Imam Bukhārī and (2) Imam Muslim are supposed to be the most authentic of all. Those by (3) Tirmizī, (4) Abu Dāu'd, (5) Abu Nasā'ī and (6) Ibn Mājah are the other four to make up the six. Another popular collection is *Mishkāt-ul-Masabīh* (=niche of lamp), which, besides containing *ahādīs* from the authentic collections, contains a few more which are held in high esteem among Muslims without actually counting as canonical. Each of these collections has a separate section devoted to the subject of *jihād*. It would require the labour of a German scholar to analyse all these collections critically. Not for the present writer such Herculean labour; the reader of this chapter must be content with citations from Imam Muslim and *Mishkāt* alone.[2]

For a full understanding of a *hadīs*, it is important to have some knowledge of its narrator. The Hadis of course records the Prophet's sayings and doings, but it does so through his Companions who, in Arabic, are designated as *Sahābah*. The Hadis in fact is a collection of first-hand reports—those proceeding from certain Companions regarding what they heard from the Prophet's own lips or what they found the Prophet doing at a certain juncture. Among these Companions, the most famous was Ayesha, the Prophet's child-wife and his favourite. The other narrators include such names as Abu Hurairah, Jabir, Anas bin Malik, Abu Sayeed, Abu Musa, the second Caliph Umar and a host of others.

What does the Hadis say on the subject of *jihād*? The most

[2] The material of the Hadis literature is almost identical whatever the collection. So the reader will not miss much by my failing from German thoroughness.

important piece of information it contains is that the Prophet, in course of his ten years' stay at Medina till his death, had engaged is as many as 82 *jihāds* of which 26 he commanded in person.[3] These 26 *jihād*s are called *ghazwahs* indicating that he became a *ghāzī* by slaying kafirs and coming out victorious. The Hadis also tell us that most of these *ghazwahs* were in the nature of raids or swooping down upon the enemy without previous notice. The Hadis also gives details regarding the vast wealth and the great number of men, women and children he captured in these *ghazwahs*. Before we give some idea of this *ghanīmah* (plunder), it is important to learn how the Koranic Revelations regarding *jihād* are confirmed by the Hadis.

(1) That *jihād* is the greatest duty of a Muslim is described in the Hadis without any scope for doubt or ambiguity. According to Imam Muslim. "It has been narrated on the authority of Abu Hurairah that the Messenger of Allah said: One who died but did not fight in the way of Allah nor did express any desire (or determination) for *Jihād* died the death of a hypocrite" (*Sahih Muslim*, No. 4696).

To get a clear understanding of this *hadīs* it is necessary, first of all, to understand the meaning of the term 'hypocrite'. The Arabic *munāfiq* which is usually used for this term has a very specialised meaning in the Koran. It refers to those people of Medina who, having given shelter to the Prophet and his followers, had gradually grown disenchanted with them because of their violence and the ruffainly character, but did not dare rise in open rebellion against them. The leader of this disaffected Medinese faction was Abdullah bin Ubayy, a name cursed and reprobated in Islam for all time to come. The Koran itself has cursed these so-called hypocrites with words of the hardest denunciation and scorn. The Hadis has announced that their reward is the lowest layer of hell—a whole layer below the one allotted to idolaters.

---

[3] The number varies from narrator to narrator.

With the background it is clear that the foregoing *hadīs* pronounces the waging of *jihād* as a Mussalman's supreme duty, failing which he is asked to cherish a fervent desire for it so that the terrible fate of a *munāfiq* does not overtake him in the hereafter. In a word, the Hadis declares even more uncomprisingly than the Koran itself that a pacifist Mussalman is not a Mussalman at all.

(2) It is clear then that the *mujāhid's* reward in the hereafter should be superior to that of a non-combant Muslim. We have seen that the Koran pronounces as much when it allots for a *mujāhid* a 'greater reward' than that for a peace-loving believer. The extent of its greatness is described in a *hadīs* as follows:

"It has been narrated on the authority of Abu Said Khudri that the Messenger of Allah said to him (Abu said): Whoever cheerfully accepts Allah as his Lord, Islam as his religion and Muhammad as his Apostle, is necessarily entitled to enter Paradise... (But) there is another act which elevates the position of a man in Paradise to a grade one hundred (higher) and the elevation between one grade and the other is equal to the height of the heaven from the earth. Abu Said said: What is that act? He replied: *Jihād* in the way of Allah! *Jihād* in the way of Allah" (*Sahih Muslim*, No. 4645).

This hadīs clearly indicates that the difference between a pacifist Mussalman and a *mujāhid* Mussalman is as great as the difference between heaven and earth—the pacifist's reward rising to no higher than earthly eminences.

(3) *Ahādīs* that refer to the blood-soaked nature of *jihād* are not rare. No. 4549 of *Mishkāt* has the followings:

"According to the venerable Abu Musa, Allah's Messenger has said: The portals of heaven lie under the shadow of the swords. On hearing this a lean and emaciated man stood up and said: O Abu Musa, did you hear this *hadīs* with your own ears? 'Yes', said Abu Musa, and then and there the man went up to his companions and said: I bid you *salaam*. So saying he broke the sheath of his Sword and proceeded towards the enemies. He killed many with that sword and ultimately attained martyrdom himself."

Clearly the sword is the Mussalman's best passport to heaven. The Prophet's own conviction comes out with singular intensity in the following *hadīs*. For those who want to set up Islam and its Prophet as devoted to the cause of peace this *hadīs* bears reading and re-reading:

"It has been narrated on the authority of Abu Hurairah who said: I heard the messenger of Allah say: I would not stay behind (when) an expedition (for *Jihād* was being mobilised) if it were (not) going to be too hard upon the believers... By the Being in whose Hand is my life, I love that I should be killed in the way of Allah; then I should be brought back to life and be killed again in His way" (*Sahih Muslim*, No. 4631).

(4) Peace and Islam are in fact wholly at variance. The Prophet's withering contempt for religions of peace comes out in the following *hadīs* and breath-taking intensity:

"Said the Venerable Abu Umama: On a certain occasion we went out with the Prophet on a campaign. One man among us was passing by a well standing by the side of a field studded with green vegetation. The spot roused in his mind a strange longing (for a life of seclusion, and he thought): How glorious would it be if I could renounce the vanities of the world and reside in this spot (for the rest of my days). He sought the permission of Allah's Messenger. Said his Highness: (Listen to me, O man of little understanding): I was not sent down (by Allah) to preach the religion of Jews and Christians. To keep oneself busy in the way of Allah for a single morning or afternoon is better than the whole earth and whatever (wealth) it possesses. And to get imprisoned in the field of battle is better than being engaged in surplus prayers for as many as 60 whole years" (*Mishkāt*, No. 4489).[5]

---

[4] Translated from a Bengali version of *Mishkāt*.

[5] Ibid.

This *hadīs* indicates that even the partial pacifism of Judaism and Christianity was not acceptable to the Prophet of Islam. In an epoch when the Christians propagated their religion with the swords, the Prophet was not agreeable to even their theoretical pacifism.

(5) Quite a few *ahādīs* bring out the fact that the pre-eminent aim of *jihād* is the expansion of Islam by war. We have already seen that this is preached in the Koran itself. The following *hadīs* not only reiterates the aim but also explains the sequence of objectives which a *mujāhid* is supposed to strive for:

"Fight in the name of Allah and the way of Allah. Fight against those who disbelieve in Allah... When you meet your enemies who are polytheists, invite them to three courses of action... Invite them to (accept) Islam... If they refuse to accept Islam, accept from them the *jizya*. If they refuse to pay the tax, seek Allah's help and fight them" (*Sahih Muslim*, No. 4294).

It is also necessary to add that, in this *hadīs* at least, the sequence does not seem to include *ghanīmah* (plunder). The triad of aims discussed here seems to exclude plunder of infidel property and enslavement of infidel population as aims of independent importance. This gap, however, is adequately filled in other *ahādīs* which will be discussed in subsequent chapters.

(6) At this point it is important to understand the meaning of two technical expressions related to *jihād*. The expression *ghāzī* I have already explained as standing for a victorious 'slayer of infidels'. But there is another expression, *shahīd* (witness), which means 'the person who attains martyrdom by offering evidence (*shahādah*) to the truth of Islam by fighting infidels'.

There are *ahādīs* describing the best manner of *shahādah* (evidence) offered by *mujāhid* who has become a martyr.

(A question arose as to) "what kind of martyrdom in *jihād* is the best. Said Allah's Messenger: When a martyr sends (an infidel's) blood streaming, he should (before falling dead) cut off the feet of the horse carrying (the said infidel)" (*Mishkāt*, No. 4530).[6]

This *hadīs* brings out the blood-lust of the *mujāhid* with perfect candour. The translator commenting on this *hadīs* says: "'Sending and infidel's blood streaming and wounding his mount'—these two items indicate the martyr's seeking of death after delivering the finishing stroke to his enemy. The emphasis here is on the *mujāhid's* realisation of his full remuneration in *jihād* in life and property." This analysis needs no further comment.

The Hadis literature has many other this to say on *jihād*. Summing up the ones I have mentioned, one can say that it retains all the injunctions of the Koran and in fact adds quite a few things more. (1) That *jihād* is the supreme duty of a Muslim is preached with greater intensity in the Hadis in the light of the Prophet's impassioned utterances regarding what may be called his 'aim of life'. (2) the objectives of Islamic expansion, *jizyah* and infidel-slaughter are enumerated in the Hadis *seriatim*,—the Koran does not mention such sequence. (3) 'the full realisation of a martyr's remuneration in life and property' is explained in the Hadis with supreme emphasis—the Koran lacks such candour, although the admonition for killing the infidel and destroying him to the uttermost limit are implicit, and sometimes explicit, in the Koran. (4) The relative pacifism of the Jews and the Christians is emphatically rejected in the Hadis—the Koran is silent on the subject.

---

[6] Ibid., *Mishkāt* has quoted this *hadīs* from the *Sahih* of Dāu'd.

3

Ghanīmah or Plunder in the Koran

To round off the theoretical discussion of *jihād* I must pass on to the doctrine of *ghanīmah* as explained in the Koran and the Hadis. We have seen that the reward of a *mujāhid* in the hereafter is the highest heaven. What is his reward on earth? It is plunder', or 'spoils of war', or 'war booty', as the Arabic expression *ghanīmah* is variously translated. Not many are prepared to believe that plunder can be considered a meritorious or even desirable outcome of the highest duty enjoined upon the followers of a religion. To remove their incredulity a somewhat detailed discussion of the matter is necessary. It has to be admitted that both the Koran and the Hadis declare this outcome of *jihād* as much inferior to the propagation of Islam as also to the pleasures of Paradise to be earned by fighting with the infidels. But at the same time these works have given detailed instructions on the mode of distribution of plunder as also the laws regulating the distribution. The legislation relating to this is first mentioned in the Koran itself. The Hadis elaborates it and narrates the Prophet's own plundering activities. Last but not the least, the various schools of Islamic jurisprudence codify the regulations in a systematic manner. I shall come to the school of jurisprudence in their proper place. Here I refer to the relevant Koranic verses which will be supported by the relevant *ahādīs* in the next chapter. But first of all I must explain the word *ghanīmah*.

As stated above, the technical meaning of *ghanīmah* is plunder or war booty, and it includes all types of booty wrested from the unbeliever—his goods, his land, his gold and silver, as also his wife and children. But the literal meaning of the word seems to be 'anything that enriches' (the victor). Etymologically the word is derived from '*ghanīm*', enemy and means that which has been got from him. But in the technical terminology of Islam, it has come to connote 'loot'. The Hadis mentions 99 alternative names of Allah, *Al-Mughnī* being one of them. That name in English means 'Enricher'. *Mughnī* is a word obviously related to *ghanīmah*. But it is doubtful if Allah is supposed to enrich his devotees by loot alone. In other words, it is quite possible that *ghanīmah* might well be an euphemism in its literal sense just as *jihād* (=effort, striving) is one. Islam has a large stock of such euphemisms, including the world 'Islam' itself which is supposed to mean 'peace'.[1] But whatever euphemism lies hidden in the word *ghanīmah*, technically it means 'plunder in *jihād*', and nothing else.[2]

It should not surprise the reader to learn that quite a few Muslim translators feel a sort of delicacy or diffidence in rendering the word *ghanīmah* as 'plunder'. Some of them use the expression 'wealth gained in war', or some such circumlocution. But the more faithful English versions everywhere render it as 'plunder', or use an equivalent expression—'spoils' being the most usual rendering. All such expressions, however, mean 'loot', pure and simple. 'Wealth gained in war' is a euphemism which conceals the real import of *ghanīmah*.

What are the injunctions regarding *ghanīmah* in the *Koran*? The eighth chapter of the Koran is entitled *Anfāl*, meaning 'surplus earning' or 'bonus'. The whole of this chapter relates to war booty which is the 'bonus' in question. The idea seems to be that the chief objective of *jihād* is Islamic expansion and the pleasures of the Paradise. Earning of spoils is merely a surplus earn-

---

[1] This meaning is wrong. 'Islam' means 'surrender' to Allah by his followers so that Allah could settle his score with non-Muslims, vide Koran 3/19.

[2] In everyday Muslim parlance, the word '*ghanīmat*' stands for 'good fortune', and sounds farthest from 'plunder obtained in a blood-thirsty war'. Even so, it retains the sense of 'bounty' or gain in the normal course.

ing—an incidental incentive to the *mujāhid's* religious zeal, so to say.

(a) The first verse of *Sūrah Anfāl* says:

"They ask thee of the spoils of war. Say: The spoils of war belong to Allah and the Messenger. So keep your duty to Allah."

The obvious meaning of this verse is that plunder is an act of charity issuing from Allah and his Prophet—no *mujāhid* should look upon it as his own earning.

But verse forty-one of the same chapter says:

"And know that whatever ye take as spoils of war, lo! a fifth thereof is for Allah and His Messenger and for the kinsmen and orphans and the needy and the wayfarer."

This verse raised a question as to the allotting of shares from the plunder; as such, it indirectly recognises some share (i.e. four-fifths) for the *mujāhids* as well.

The important thing about this one-fifth of the plunder is that Islamic scholars call it the 'holy one-fifth'. The technical expression for it is *Khums*, otherwise spelt as *Khams*. According to the schools of jurisprudence, this one-fifth is to proceed to the Muslim king's treasury when the Prophet is no more. A similar word is *Fai* which stands for the whole plunder going to the Prophet (or the Sultan) if it is obtained without regular warfare. *Jizyah* itself is a sort of *Fai*—the Prophet or the Sultan being the sole owner of that gain.

(b) Who then is to own the remaining four-fifths of the plunder obtained by a regular campaign? Should that be given away to the whole body of Muslims? The Koran says: No Mussalman except the *mujāhid* is entitled to any share of the four-fifths. Allah says clearly:

"Those who were left behind will say: When ye set forth to capture booty, let us go with you. Say: Ye shall not go with us" (K 48/15).

Historically this verse refers to certain Arab tribes around Medina, who had been called by the Prophet to join his expedition to Hudaibiyah (628 AD) but who chose to stay behind. They were to get no share of the booty, enjoined Allah.

(c) Whether it be a bonus or Allah's bounty to the believers who engaged in *jihād*, Allah's pledge to lead the believers to adequate plunder is also available in the Koran:

"Allah was well pleased with the believers when they swore allegiance unto thee (i.e. the Prophet) beneath the tree, and He knew what was in their hearts and He sent down peace of reassurance on them, and hath rewarded them with a near victory; and much booty they will capture" (K 48/18-19).

Historically this verse refers to the famous Pledge of the Tree which the followers of the Prophet took at Hudaibiyah, when a rumour was circulated that the Prophet's emissary to the Meccans, his son-in-law Othman (later on the future Caliph), had been killed by the latter. Allah's 'peace of reassurance' was accompanied with intimation regarding adequate plunder awaiting the faithful in near future.

(d) Such reward was not promised to Mussalmans of the Prophet's time alone. His followers for all time to come would continue to receive booty:

"And other (gain) which ye have not been able to achieve, Allah will compass it" (K 48/21).

In other words, plunder is every *mujāhid's* birthright—it is a never ceasing dispensation.

(e) Supposing that a *mujāhid* of tender conscience refuses to acquire booty? Says Allah:

"Eat ye the spoils of war. They are lawful and pure" (K 8/69).[3]

This verse shows that Allah exonerates the plundering Mussalmans from all misgivings arising from the prickings of conscience.

(f) The Koran is not given to circumstantial references to historical events. But the plundering of the Jewish clan of Kuraizah

---

[3] This rendering is by Abdul Hamid Siddiqi.

supposed to have been in league with the Meccans in the Battle of Ahzāb (627 AD) is mentioned there in some detail:

"And (Allah) brought those of the people of Scripture who supported (the Meccans) from their strongholds, and cast panic into their hearts. Some ye slew and ye made captive some. And he caused you to inherit their lands and their houses and their wealth" (K 33/26-27).

Land, houses, wealth, captives! The nature of *ghanīmah* is made explicit in this verse.

Of such plunder, the male population (chiefly children) are enslaved, and the females inducted in the *mujāhids'* harems when not sold out in the slave market. The Koran elaborates the right of the *mujāhid* over captured kafir women.

"And all married woman are (forbidden unto you) save those (captives) whom your right hands possess" (K 4/24).

In this verse, the character of *ghanīmah* is explained with brutal frankness. The captured kafir women, snatched from their husbands, can be enjoyed with absolute impunity by the *mujāhids*. True, the Koarn does not spell out the nature of the indulgence. But its decree regarding kafir women possessed by the *mujāhid's* right hand is obviously not one of honourable re-marriage. It is nothing but forcible concubinage. Lest there should be any doubt regarding the nature of the indulgence, the Hadis adds its own tell-tale gloss upon this very verse. I shall take up this gloss in the next chapter. Here a summary of the contents of the chapters is in order.

In brief, the property of the infidel—his wealth, his women and children—, all without exception, is lawful plunder for the *mujāhid*. The merit of such plunder is indeed less than that of spreading Islam and looking up to the pleasures of the other world, but the Koran has given it due recognition. Not only that. It has explained the mode of its disposal as between *mujāhid* and *mujāhid*, and also as between the *mujāhid* and his commander. Not only that. It has, in unmistakable language, pronounced the plunder 'lawful' and 'pure'.

4

Plunder (*Ghanīmah*) in the Hadis

(1) Is plunder compatible with religion and piety? We have seen that the Koran itself says 'yes'. But it appears that some objection was raised against this view as early as the Prophet's own life-time. The Prophet himself met this objection in a somewhat longish *hadīs*. We find him declaring in favour of the Koranic view by contrasting Allah's dispensation regarding plunder in the epoch of former prophets with that in his own. The same issue had been raised when the followers of a former prophet had amassed a goodly amount of loot which Allah apparently disapproved. So "a fire approached the spoils to devour them", but stopped just short of touching it. The prophet of aforetime was cleaver enough to guess the reason for such strange behaviour on the part of the divine fire. And he told his followers, "One of you must be guilty of concealing a part of the spoil. So come forward and touch my hand by way of swearing fealty to me." One or two hands stuck the prophet's hand and, true enough, on questioning they disgorged "gold equal in volume to the head of a cow". So the whole plunder was put together and Allah's fire promptly lapped it up. To the prophet of Islam, the meaning of this parable was unmistakable. As he reasoned:

"The spoils of war were not made lawful for any people before us. This is because Allah saw our weakness and humility and made them lawful for us" (*Sahih Muslim*, No.4327).

(2) It should be clear from the foregoing episode that the Hadis makes its own addition to the Koranic doctrine of *ghanīmah*. The *mujāhid* must despoil the infidel as a matter of

course, but he should not 'misappropriate' any portion of the loot. The plunder is property of the Islamic state so long as it is not doled out to each according to his performance, the Prophet's (or the Sultan's) 'holy one fifth' being the pick of the basket. Keeping the plunder for oneself without reference to the commander is a grievous sin. As the Prophet puts it in another *hadīs*:

"Fight against those who disbelieve in Allah. Make a holy war; do not embezzle the spoils" (*Sahih Muslim*, No. 4294).

In fact, 'embezzlement of spoils' is one of the deadliest sins in Islam. This comes out in a number of *ahādīs*. A slave of the Prophet was killed in *jihād* against the Jews of Khaibar (AD 628). When people started greeting him as a martyr, the Prophet cried out:

"Nay, not so. By Him in Whose hand is the life of Muhammad, the small garment he stole on the day of Khaibar but which did not fall to his lot is burning like the Fire (of Hell) on him" (*Sahih Muslim*, No. 210).

(3) I have said that this doctrine of embezzlement or misappropriation of the spoils is a addition to the Koanic doctrine of plunder made by the Prophet on his own. But it must be understood that what the Hadis has added to the Koran is but a logical corollary. Plunder, this side of religion, is a vocation natural to robbers. If Robbers go on a plundering spree, it is only the iron discipline of the leader that prevents them from falling out among themselves for a larger share of the gain. Now if one were to invoke divine sanction for the plunder, one must similarly make provision for divine disapproval against its misappropriation. The two things hang together, and what the Hadis has added is only a legitimate extension of the Koran.

(4) The Hadis has made many other additions to the doctrine of *ghanīmah*. It would be tedious to enumerate all of them, but one important addition, equally logical, merits mentioning. "The Messenger of Allah allotted two shares from the spoils to the horseman and one share to the footman" (*Sahih Muslim*, Nos. 4358-59). The learned Pakistani translator of Imam Muslim

refers to the vast Islamic literature which expounds this tenet and he himself breaks into lyricism in extolling such beauties of the Hadis.

(5) A far more important extension made by the Hadis to the doctrine of *ghanīmah* is the inclusion of the whole world as the Mussalman's rightful 'field of spoliation' so to say. The Koran speaks of the "other gain which the Muslims have not yet been able tot achieve" (K 48/21). The Hadis tells us that the "whole of earth belongs to Allah and His Apostle". Because such *ahādīs* touch the issue of Islamising the whole of humanity this *hadīs* merit quoting *in extenso*. But first of all a preliminary word.

The reader should know that early Islam became prosperous by destroying one by one the Jewish settlements around Medina and wresting their lands and goods and women and children as plunder. A *hadīs* refers to the this practice of spoliation with absolute candour and incidentally brings out the theory of wholesale Islamisation of humanity. The *Sahih Muslim* narrated on the authority of Abu Hurairah:

"We were sitting in the mosque when the Messenger of Allah came and said: Let us go to the Jews. We went out with him until we came to them. The Messenger of Allah stood up and called out to them: O ye assembly of Jews, accept Islam and you will be safe" (No. 4363).

This last sentence has been called the "communication of the messages" (of Islam) and, as has been explained previously, this is the best mode of inaugurating a *jihād*. The *hadīs* then indicates that the Jews were not agreeable to the call. The Prophet repeated the call three times consecutively and failing a satisfactory response said:

"You should know that the earth belongs to Allah and His Prophet, and I wish that I should expel you from this land" (*Ibid*).

In other words, the whole earth is the *mujāhid's* field of spoliation. The Hadis has not minced matters, but divulged the supreme mission of Islam with absolute frankness.

(6) As the last item of Hadis' addition to the Koranic doctrine of *ghanīmah*, we may mention the treatment meted out to the female captives whom the *mujāhid's* 'right hand possesses'. As mentioned in the previous chapter, they are subjected to unrestricted concubinage. The following *hadīs* brings this out without a vestige of vagueness or obscurity:

"At the battle of Hunain, Allah's Messenger sent an army to Autas... Having overcome (the infidels) and taken them captive the Companions of Allah's Messenger seemed to refrain from having intercourse with the captive women because of their husbands being polytheists. Then Allah, Most High, sent down regarding that: Forbidden unto you are the women already married except those whom your right hand possesses" (*Sahih Muslim*, No. 3432).[1]

In fine, the infidel's wealth, women and children—all are lawful plunder for the *mujāhid*. (1) To enjoy such plunder is glorious, if only less glorious than propagating Islam or contemplating the pleasures of the hereafter. The Koran proclaims its lawfulness and sanctity. The Hadis extends the Koranic message. The Hadis particularly dwells on it as a sort of special dispensation denied to former prophets. (2) The spoliation of Jews is elaborated in the Hadis as an earnest of Islam's mission over the whole earth. (3) The matter of "those whom one's right hand possesses" is explained in the Hadis with breath-taking candour.

---

[1] Koran 4/24. The Arabic phrase for "those whom your right hand possesses" is "*ma malakat ayman u kum*".

5

Islamic Expansion through *Jihād*: The Evidence of the Sunnah

In the foregoing chapters I have attempted to give a brief but complete outline of the Islamic theory of *jihād*, that is, the injunctions of Allah and his Prophet regarding the subject. However, no part of Islamic theory is supposed to be complete without a description of the Prophet's own actions in terms to those injunctions. In fact, these actions in their totality are the Sunnah properly so called, the mere injunctions even from the Prophet's mouth being only a part of it. To a devout Muslim, the Prophet's actions and sayings rather than revelations from Allah supply the model of excellence which he is expected to emulate throughout his life-span. The Prophet is the best ruler, the best parent, the best husband, and, by the same token, the best *mujāhid*. To round off the theory of *jihād*, a discussion of his own *jihād*s is, therefore, essential.

Adding up the evidence of the Koran and the Hadis, a complete *jihād* is seen to have no less than five distinct objectives: (1) Forcible spreading of Islam. (2) Destruction of the kafir population against which the *jihād* is mounted. (3) Imposition of *jizyah* on the defeated infidels. (4) The wresting of war booty in the form of material property. (5) The enslavement of the female and child population of the vanquished kafir enemy. The last two items, indeed, do not count as two, but are aspects of the selfsame *ghanīmah*. It is for clarity that they are mentioned separately. In this chapter I will concentrate on the first objective of *jihād*, namely, the spread of Islam through *jihād* as illustrated in the Prophet's own career.

This spreading of Islam through *jihād* again has two sides: to force the vanquished infidels into professing Islam, and to destroy their places as well as symbols of worship. The Koranic injunctions, in so far as they refer to forcible spread of Islam, have already been quoted. The reader should particularly refer to verses 9/5, 8/39, 2/193. The relevant Sunnah is the best described in *The Life of Mahomet* by Sir William Muir by comparing and collating the early biographical data from Ibn Ishāq, Ibn Hishām, Al-Wāqidī, Ibn Sa'd and At-Tabarī.[1] The Prophet's Sunnah regarding the spread of Islam by means of *jihād* is described in these works in great detail.

According to Muir, the Prophet never made a concerted effort for the spread of Islam in Arabia before the conquest of Mecca (January, 630 AD). He was content to keep together the band of his followers in Medina and with their help wage incessant war against the Koriesh of Mecca and other Arab tribes, so as to add to his resources and build a well-equipped military machine. The moment he felt strong enough, he swooped down on Mecca and gained what was for all practical purposes a bloodless victory. The Meccans professed Islam, intimidated as they were by the display of his strength and also because of the unwritten agreement he had reached earlier with the Meccan leader, Abu Sufyan. Muir has given a graphic description of this agreement.

According to him, the Prophet, with an army of 10,000, was proceeding towards Mecca in extreme secrecy when a small reconnoitring party of the Koreish, headed by Abu Sufyan, fell in with Al-Abbas, the Prophet's uncle, issuing forth from the latter's encampment. Al-Abbas wanted 'to save Mecca from destruction.' He persuaded Abu Sufyan to accompany him to the Prophet and 'seek quarter from him'. This was in the evening

---

[1] Ibn Ishāq (85 A.H - 151 A.H); Ibn Hishām (d. 218 A.H.); Al-Wāqidī (130 A.H-207 A.H); Ibn Sa'd (d. 230 A.H.); At-Tabarī (d. 310 A.H).

prior to the surrender of Mecca. Next morning, Al-Abbas took Abu Sufyan to the Prophet. What took place is the best described in Muir's language:

"'*Out upon thee Abu Sufyan*!' exclaimed Mohammad as the Koreishite chief drew near; '*hast thou not discovered that there is no God save the Lord alone*?' 'Noble and generous Sire! Had there been any God beside, verily he had been of some avail to me.' '*And dost thou not acknowledge that I am the Prophet of the Lord*?' questioned Mohammad. 'Nobel Sire! As to this thing there is yet in my heart some hesitancy.' Woe is thee!' exclaimed Al-Abbas; 'it is no time for this hesitancy. Believe and testify forthwith the creed of Islam, or else thy neck shall be in danger!''

This description by Muir makes it clear that Abu Sufyan professed Islam under duress—to 'save his neck from danger'. Most of the Meccans followed him in the same course and obviously under the same predicament. Muir has praised the Prophet's extreme generosity in letting off the Koriesh so easily, and abstaining from bloodshed and plunder. But he has not concealed the fact that the conversion of the Koriesh was effected by terror, by an apprehension relating to 'safety of their necks'.

It must be admitted that the generosity of the Prophet extended even beyond sparing the life and property of the Koreish. He did not compel each and every Meccan to profess Islam at once, nor threw out anyone who would persist in 'infidelity' for some time yet. They were even allowed to worship at the Ka'bah, the so-called Inviolable Place of Worship. He got the idols in the Ka'bah destroyed on the very first day of his entry into Mecca, but retained much of the pre-Islamic rituals. This facilitated for some more time the continuance of pre-Islamic worship by the as yet unconverted Koreishites, without encountering opposition from the Prophet's followers.

That opposition came about a year later (631 AD) on the occasion of the first independent pilgrimage to the Ka'bah by the Prophet's followers form Medina. At first the Prophet had sent

Abu Bakr as the leader of this pilgrimage. But after the latter had already proceeded some distance, the Prophet dispatched Ali (his cousin as well as son-in law) with a set of newly received Revelations from Allah. They were the so-called 'Immunity Verses'. By means of these, Allah gave to himself and his Prophet immunity from the responsibility for tolerating those Meccans and other Arabs who had been persisting in infidelity even after the conquest of Mecca. The *Sūrah Taubah* of the Koran contains these 'Immunity Verses', the *sūrah* itself bearing the alternative title, *Barā'ah* (immunity). Allah declared:

"Freedom from obligation from Allah and His Messenger towards those of the idolaters with whom ye made treaty.

"Travel [O idolaters] freely in the land for four months, and know that ye cannot escape Allah and Allah will confound the disbelievers.

'And a proclamation from Allah and His Messenger to all men on the day of the Greater Pilgrimage that Allah is free from obligation to idolaters and (so is) His messenger" (K 9/1-3).

It is on this occasion that the liberty to kill the idolaters ("kill them whenever you find them", K/95) was proclaimed and the doors of the Ka'bah were closed for all time to come to non-Muslims. As the "proclamation from Allah" clearly states, the unbelievers (of Arabia and not of Mecca alone) were given only four months' time to forswear their ancestral religion and profess Islam. Clearly this was a direct outcome of the conquest of Mecca although delayed after the day of victory for about a year. This therefore, must be reckoned the supreme example of how *jihād* is utilised for the forcible spread of Islam. Every practice of the Prophet is canonical Sunnah to the believer and as binding as the verses of the Koran. It is for this reason that with Muslims, *jihād* became the supreme instrument for propagating Islam and its spread by peaceful means always remained secondary. The ordinance which was originally intended for Arab idolaters, came to be recognised in due course as including idolaters anywhere and everywhere.

6

Destruction of Idols and Idol-Temples in *Jihād:* The Evidence of the Sunnah

A natural and in fact inevitable consequence of spreading Islam by *jihād* is the destruction of non-believers' places of worship and their idols. It is somewhat remarkable that this duty has not been enjoined in any Koranic verse as a part of *jihād.* The destruction of idols is often mentioned in the Koran, but nowhere in connection with *jihād.* Such an ordinance derives from the Sunnah and the Sunnah alone. In the Koran there are descriptions of such destruction in heaven at the hands of angels *(firishtas)* and on earth at the hands of Prophet Ibrāhīm (Abraham), who is proclaimed the first Mussalman in the world. But these descriptions are not connected with any *jihād.*

(1) The *sūrah* for the destruction of idols and images is *Sūrah Sāffāt,* the 37th chapter of the Koran. This *sūrah* tells us that on the Day of Judgement Allah would assemble idols and idol-worshippers through his *firishtas* and throw them into the everlasting fire of hell. As the Koran puts it:

"(And it is said unto the angels) assemble those who did wrong, together with their wives and what (idols) they used to worship instead of Allah, and lead them to the path of hell ... Then lo! this day they (both) are sharers in the doom. Thus deal We with the guilty" (K 37/22, 23, 33, 39).

(2) So much for the destruction of idols by Allah himself through his heavenly hosts. As regards Prophet Ibrāhīm's hand in the matter, the Koran describes his iconoclasm in several passages, notably in the same *sūrah* 37 as also in *sūrah* 21

(Anbiyā). In the former this is how Ibrāhīm proceeded in regard to the deities of his kinsmen:

"Ibrahim said unto his father and his folk: What is it that ye worship? Is it a falsehood—gods beside Allah—that ye desire?... And he glanced a glance at the stars; then said: Lo! I feel sick. And they turned their backs and went away from him. Then turned he to their gods and said: Will ye not eat? What aileth ye that ye speak not? Then he attacked them striking with his right hand. And his people came towards him hastening. He said: Worship ye that ye yourselves carve?" (K 37/85ff).

Such are the Koranic accounts of the destruction of idols. It appears that what Ibrāhīm objected to was his folk's addiction to 'false gods' who could not 'eat or speak'. To us this does not constitute so serious an offence as to rouse one to iconoclastic fury. However, the Koran does not mention if, beyond striking his folk's idols behind their back, Ibrāhīm waged any full-*fledged jihād* against his idolatrous kinsmen. That was left to the Prophet of Islam who in his *jihād* against his kinsmen destroyed all the idols in and around the Ka'bah and signalled the event as a permanent legacy to future *mujāhids*.

According to the account given by all biographers of the Prophet, on reaching Mecca, he mounted his camel Al-Kaswa and proceeded towards the Ka'bah. On reaching there he saluted the famous Black Stone with his staff and made seven circuits round the sacred building. "Then pointing with his staff to the idols one by one, he commanded them to be hewn down." The huge idol of Hubal stood in front of the temple. As the Prophet's followers attacked it with pickaxes the image fell down with a crash. The Prophet celebrated its fall by shouting a verse from the Koran: "Truth hath come and falsehood gone, for falsehood verily vanisheth away" (K 17/81).

This was not all. The destruction of Hubal was followed by the destruction of all the pictures decorating the walls of the temple. An announcer was asked to go down the streets of Mecca shouting a proclamation: "Whoever believeth in Allah, let him not leave in his house any image whatever that he doth not break in pieces." The fury of idol-breaking was unleashed in the city.

In the next two weeks the Prophet despatched his armed squads to all places in the neighbourhood with the express command to destroy the images as also their shrines. Khālid destroyed the fane of Al-Uzzā at Nakhla. Amr smashed the image of Suwā' worshipped by the tribe of Hudhail. Al-Manāt was destroyed at Kodeid. This particular work of destruction was entrusted to a tribe of Medina who had been specially attached to this deity. This was the Prophet's way of testing their zeal for Islam.

Muir's description of the destruction of the image of Al-Lāt, worshipped by the Thakif tribe of Taif, is particularly touching. Following close upon the conquest of Mecca the Prophet had besieged the city of Taif, but the siege had to be raised because of the heroic resistance of the Thakafites. But when every surrounding tribe started professing Islam and organising raid upon raid against them, the Thakafites decided to offer submission. Their attachment to their Goddess Al-Lāt, however, was too strong to be renounced so easily. Already they had killed one of their own chiefs, Urwa, who, having professed Islam on his own, would have all his fellow-citizens follow in his footsteps. But harassed and exhausted by Islamic attacks from all sides they at last sent out a deputation of six chiefs who pleaded with the Prophet for retaining the temple of Al-Lāt for another three years even after professing Islam. As was to be expected, the Prophet rejected the plea. Thereafter they prayed for a respite of two years, one year, six months, successively with tearful supplication. The Prophet was stubborn in his refusal, declaring that Al-Lāt could not coexist with Allah for a single day. The only concession the Thakafites could get was that they were not required to destroy the image of Al-Lāt with their own hands. Al-Mughira, a kinsman to Urwa, and Abu Sufyan, the Koreishite leader, volunteered to perform that task. "Al-Mughira, wielding a pickaxe and surrounded by a guard of his relatives, and amid the cries and wailing of the women, with his own hand, hewed [the image] to the ground."

"A Christian with iconoclastic tendencies himself, Muir has wasted few words of sympathy for the people whose Gods and shrines were so ruthlessly destroyed. But even he seems to have been somewhat affected by the devotion of the Thakafites to their deity. As he puts it, "Al-Taif was the last stronghold that held out against the authority of Mohammad. It is remarkable as the only place where the fate of an idol excited the sympathy of the people. Everywhere else the images seem to have been destroyed by the people themselves without a pang." We can ignore the last sentence as proceeding from the pen of a would-be iconoclast, but the heartless manner of trampling upon the devotion of the Thakafites as illustrated in the above incident is an eloquent commentary on the virtue of breaking other people's idols.

But whatever be one's opinion about this vandalism, the Islamic significance of these events can hardly be exaggerated. Iconoclasm became part and parcel of *jihād* not by any specific injunction of the Koran but by the very activities following upon the conquest of Mecca. These constituted the Prophet's Sunnah and was an addition to the teachings of the Koran, so much so that in a great many *jihāds* waged by the latter-day zealots of Islam, the very words which the Prophet had uttered at the time of destroying the image of Hubal at Ka'bah became a part of the ritual of iconoclasm unleashed at the end of a successful *jihād:* "Truth hat come and falsehood gone; for verily falsehood vanisheth away."

7

Slaughter of Infidels in *Jihād*: The Evidence of the Sunnāh

The generosity shown by the Prophet to his kinsmen at Mecca was not matched by anything in relation to the Jews of Medina, nor, for the matter of that, to any Jewish tribe of Arabia. Actually, the Prophet's uniformly stringent measures adopted against the Jews contrasted most signally with his leniency towards the Arabs. To account for the contrast, D.S. Margoliouth credits the Prophet with being a "champion of the national idea" of the Arabs, and this supposition does give a national explanation of his uniform hostility to the Jews. As Margoliouth puts it, "With this attitude [namely the Prophet's supposed nationalism] agreed his ordinary tenderness for the lives of Arabs when he massacred Jews without mercy." Whatever the explanation, the Prophet's treatment of the Jews brings out a most important body of Sunnah connected with one aspect of *jihād,* namely, "making slaughter in the land" (K 8/67). To illustrate this aspect, a short account of the massacre of the Jewish clan of Kuraizah is in order.

This event had taken place three whole years before the conquest of Mecca, and it may be said that the Sunnah regarding slaughter of infidels in *jihād* had been well established by it, so that the Prophet's lenient treatment of the Meccans was an exception designed to prove the rule. To understand the rule clearly, we must remember that the destruction of Banu Kuraizah was an episode connected with the Battle of the Ditch. This battle took place in 627 AD following a siege of Medina by a body of the

Koreish and sundry other tribes. By that time Banu Kuraizah had been left as the only considerable Jewish tribe in Medina, those of Banu Kainuka and Banu Nazir having been banished a few years previously. It was alleged by most of the early Muslim writers that Banu Kuraizah were in league with the Koreish and this opinion has been broadly accepted by most of the latter-day scholars. The Jews did not in fact participate in the battle, but their hostile movements kept the Muslim army on tenterhooks during the month-long siege. As soon as the siege was raised, the angel Gabriel is said to have visited the Prophet and asked him to punish the "traitors" immediately without thinking of rest or repose. As a *hadīs* puts it:

"Gabriel said: you have laid down arms. By God, we haven't laid them down. So march against them. The Messenger of Allah asked: Where? He pointed to the Banu Quraiza" *(Sahih Muslim,* No. 4370).

What transpired after this is easily described. The Prophet laid siege to the stronghold of Banu Kuraizah, who were starved into suing for submission. The Jews offered to face banishment leaving their property behind. The Prophet did not agree. They appealed for mediation by the Arab tribe of Aus of which they were clients. The Prophet agreed to this and asked the Ausite chief, Sa'd bin Muā'z, to administer judgement. Sa'd pronounced the verdict in the name of Allah. All male members of the Kuraizah (barring children) were to be put to death, their women and children were to be sold into slavery, and their property was to be distributed among Muslims. The Prophet praised Sa'd as having "adjudged the case with the judgment of God, the Exalted and Glorified".[1]

The slaughter of Banu Kuraizah sheds a lurid light on the early annals of Islam. A big pit was dug in the market place of Medina, and 800 Jews (according to Muir's calculation) were brought down, chained and manacled, to be beheaded in cold

---

[1] *Sahih Muslim.*

blood. The Prophet himself presided over the massacre. The able-bodied prisoners were brought in companies of five or six, seated in a row on the brink of the pit, and beheaded in a leisurely manner, their bodies being cast into the pit. A women whose husband had just perished, admitted to having killing a Muslim by throwing a big stone during the siege and, having refused the gift of life granted to the enslaved womenfolk, was promptly despatched at her own request. Her smiling face as she stepped forward for execution is said to have haunted the Prophet's child-wife Ayesha to the end of her days.[2] The Kuraizah showed signal courage in facing death, but for Islam the punishment meted out to them merely constituted the canonical precedent for "making slaughter in the land".

It must be mentioned that barring Muir few European scholars have found fault with the Prophet for the gruesome murder of the men of Banu Kuraizah. According to D.S. Magoliouth "Those who had taken part openly with the invaders of Medina could not very well be permitted to remain there. To banish them was unsafe; to permit them to remain was yet more dangerous. Hence they must die... And since it would appear that the Kuraizah had turned against the Prophet merely because he was in extreme danger, their fate, horrible as it was, does not surprise us. If they had not succeeded in harming him, they had manifested the will to do so.

More recently a French scholar, Maxime Rodinson, has defended the Prophet in stronger language. As he puts it, "from a purely political point of view, the massacre was an extremely wise move. The chosen solution was undeniably the best."

The Muslim apologist Syed Amir Ali too has defended the Prophet. He argues that as the Jews themselves had wanted the Ausites to arbitrate, no question of blaming the Prophet can possibly arise.

---

[2] This indicates that the women of Medina had been invited to feast their eyes upon the gruesome spectacle.

It is not necessary to comment on these judgments pronounced by latter-day critics. But the reader must be reminded of one thing even at the risk of tiresome repetition. To the devout followers of Islam, the massacre of Banu Kuraizah is part of the Prophet's Sunnah. It is not as if the matter ended with the slaughter that took place in 627 AD in the market place of Medina. Over the centuries, the *mujāhids* have been inspired by this part of the Sunnah to emulate the Prophet in similar massacres of the infidels. Timur at Delhi, towards the close of the 14th century, followed the Prophet's seventh century exploit at Medina by murdering in cold blood *one hundred thousand* Hindu prisoners captured by him during his prolonged *jihād.* A devout follower of the Koran and the Sunnah he "made slaughter in the land" rather than seek ransom for his helpless victims. It is not the 800 Jews of Medina, but the millions of infidels slaughtered in subsequent centuries that should make us pause and reflect. Not only that. Those who defend the Prophet should reflect on the fate of the millions of infidels for whose heads the *mujāhid's* knife is being sharpened in all Islamic countries right at this moment.

8

Plunder (*Ghanīmah*) in *Jihād*: The Evidence of the Sunnah

Did the Prophet appropriate plunder (*ghanīmah*) for his own use? The relevant Revelations and *ahādīs* have already been discussed in detail, and the part of *Khums*, the holy one-fifth of the plunder in the Islamic scheme of things, analysed threadbare. But here again the Prophet's own practice (*Sunnah*) has to be mentioned if only to round off the discussion. A proper analysis of this single topic would require a whole book; here I shall content myself with a bare outline.

(1) According to the biographers, the Prophet received his one-fifth starting from the raid of Nakhla (late 623 AD) in which one Koreishite was killed and two of them made captives, the booty obtained being meagre. But as the earliest of the Prophet's biographers, Ibn Ishāq, reflected, "This was the first booty which the Muslims obtained, the first captives they seized, and the first life they took." The amount of ransom money charged was 40 ounces of silver for each of the two captured Koreishites.

(2) In comparison, the loot from the Battle of Badr (624 AD) was considerable. Besides a vast amount of garments and articles of leather, the number of camels captured was 114 and that of horses 10, the captive Koreishites totalling 70.[1] According to Margoliouth's calculation, the ransom money charged was 100,000 *dirhems*. The Prophet received a clear one-fifth of these.

[1] These are Sir William Muir's figures. Margoliouth says that the camels numbered 150.

Over and above, he took the camel of Abu Jahl,[2] his most inveterate Koreishite enemy happily "sent to hell" on the battlefield, as also the famous sword Zulfiqār. These constituted his special share as the chief of his team.

(3) The largest amount of plunder earned during the Prophet's ten years' residence at Medina was obtained at the cost of the Jews. A short account of these earnings should elucidate the relevant Sunnah for plunder with more vividness than any other event could.

As is well known, the Prophet's conquering career started with his migration to Medina in September 622 AD. In the history of Islam the event is known as the Migration (*hijrah*) with a capital M. The Prophet's previous career of 12 or 13 years' preaching at Mecca had enlisted very few converts. In Medina, indeed he was received with the honour due to a monarch, but this was not accompanied by any accession of wealth or property. The first gainful exploit of Muslims was the victory of Badr. But the plunder obtained therefrom, though opulent, was not considerable enough to feed the growing Muslim population indefinitely. It seems to be this consideration above any other which actuated the Prophet for extirpating the thriving Jewish settlements around Medina and attaching their property to the nascent Islamic state. It has been argued that the Jews themselves had behaved treacherously with him. But if "all earth belongs to Allah and His Prophet" such a rationalisation is hardly necessary. In any event, after the victory of Badr the Jewish tribes of Medina started being a prey to the Prophet's repeated assaults. Banu Kainuka was the first tribe to be thrown out. This event occurred close on the heels of Badr. After the reverse at Uhud (625 AD), it was the turn of the Banu Nazir to be banished. Banu Kuraizah, as mentioned earlier, were exterminated after the Battle of Ahzāb (627 AD). All these were Jewish tribes of Medina.

---

[2] His real name was Abu Hakm (father of wisdom). But as he was resolutely opposed to Islam, the Prophet named him Abu Jahl (father of folly).

The very next year saw the raid upon Khaibar (628 AD), that is, on the Jews who resided far from Medina. They were retained in their settlements on condition of tilling their own lands and paying half their produce to the Islamic state. This seems to be the first imposition of *jizyah* in the history of Islam. The extirpation or subjugation of Jews in all these cases was followed by extortion of a vast amount of *ghanīmah* (plunder).

(a) Property worth thousands of *dirhems*, if not more, accrued from the expulsion of Banu Nazir (625 AD). This tribe had rich and extensive agricultural lands, all of which was appropriated by the Prophet. This was because the Nazirites were conquered without engaging in regular warfare, so that their property was counted as *Fai* (gift) in Islam's technical vocabulary.[3] As Abdul Hamid Siddiqi's commentary on a *hadīs* elaborates:

"The properties abandoned by Banu Nazir were the ones which Allah bestowed upon his Apostle for which no expedition was taken either with cavalry or camel. Those properties were particularly meant for the Holy Prophet. He would meet the annual expenditure of his family from the income thereof and would spend what remained for purchasing horses and weapons for preparation of *Jihād*" (*Sahih Muslim*, No. 4347).

(b) The plunder accruing from the extermination of the entire male population of Banu Kuraizah is best described in Muir's language. As he puts it:

"The booty was divided into four classes—lands, chattels, cattle and slaves; and Mohammad took a fifth of each. There were (besides the children who counted with their mothers) a thousand captives; from his share of these, Mohammad made certain presents to his friends of slave girls and female servants. The rest of the women and children he sent to be sold among the Bedawi tribes of Nejd, in exchange for horses and arms in the

[3] *Fai* is Koranic rather than Prophetic. "And that which Allah gave as spoil to his Messenger from them, ye urged not any horse or camel for the sake thereof. But Allah giveth lordship to His Messenger over whom He will" (K 59/6).

service of the State; for he kept steadily in view the advantage of raising a body of efficient cavalry. The remaining property was divided among the 3,000 soldiers of Medīna, to the highest bidders among whom the women also were sold.

"The whole booty at the prize valuation would thus be 40,000 dīnārs. Mohammad sold a number of State slaves to 'Othmān and 'Abd-ar-Rahmān, who made a good speculation therefrom. They divided them into old and young. 'Othmān took the old, and found as he expected much money on their persons. Large sums were obtained from the Jews of Kheibar and other places for the ransom of such of the women and children as they were interested in."[4]

This single example brings out the Prophet's practice regarding *ghanīmah* (plunder) with a vividness which a hundred pages of theoretical discussion would hardly equal.

(c) But even this booty, vast as it was, was small compared to what the Prophet wrested from the Jews of Khaibar. After their defeat, "When the Moslems came to apportion their spoils they found that the conquest of Khaibar surpassed every other benefit that God had conferred on their Prophet. The leader's one-fifth enabled him to enrich his wives and concubines, his daughters and their off-spring, his friends and acquaintance, down to the servants. Eighteen hundred lots were portioned out for the fourteen hundred fighters; the two hundred horsemen got, according to custom, treble lots ... Moreover there was no fear of this wealth melting away as the former booty had melted; for the Jews remained to till the land which became the property of the robbers."[5]

Did the Prophet appropriate female slaves in conformity with the Koranic injunction[6] on concubinage? Biographers mention Raihāna, the Jewess of Banu Kuraizah, chosen by the Prophet as his concubine after she had refused to espouse Islam, that being

[4] *The Life of Mahomet*, p. 320 and n.

[5] D.S. Margoliouth, *Mohammed and the Rise of Islam*, pp. 361-62.

[6] K 4/24; also see above.

the condition for legal marriage. But Raihāna's story does not figure prominently in the canonical *ahādīs*, which, while mentioning nine wives (apart from the long-deceased Khadija) and two concubines, dilate only on Maria, the handsome Coptic slave girl presented to the Prophet by the Christian governor of Egypt. It is not clear why Maria, who had apparently turned Muslim, was not given the benefit of legal marriage. That she was a slave could be no objection, for the Prophet could well have manumitted her. In fact, canonical *ahādīs* refer to the similar case of Safiyya with much fanfare. As Muslim writers make much of this case and cite it as an example of the Prophet's noble heart, I will describe it in some detail.

Safiyya's father Huyayya belonged to Banu Nazir. After the expulsion of his tribe from Medina, he had taken refuge at Khaibar, and, because of his warlike activities, had been assassinated by killers sent by the Prophet with an express order. Her husband Kināna was cruelly tortured and murdered in cold blood after the conquest of Khaibar, again by the Prophet's express order. In the distribution of spoils, Safiyya actually fell to the lot of Dihya, a handsome Muslim, in whose shape Gabriel is said to have often visited the Prophet. The full story is told by Imam Muslim on the authority of Anas, the Prophet's personal attendant. As Anas relates:

"We took the territory of Khaibar by force. There came Dihya and he said: Messenger of Allah, bestow upon me a girl out of the prisoners. He said: Go and get any girl. He made a choice of Safiyya. There came a person to Allah's Apostle and said: Safiyya is worthy of you only ... When Allah's Apostle saw her he said [to Dihya]: Take any other woman from among the prisoners ... He then granted her emancipation and then married her... On the way Umm Sulaim embellished and then sent her to the Holy Prophet at night. Allah's Apostle appeared as a bridegroom in the morning" (*Sahih Muslim*, No.3325).

This narrative tells its own story in the simplest language possible. But to illustrate how devout Muslims view such examples of Sunnah, one more word is necessary. Imam Muslim himself has entered this *hadīs* in his collection, not as an example of *ghanīmah* (plunder) earned by the Prophet from his *ghazwah* (expedition) but as an instance of the high morality involved in emancipating a slave woman before marrying her! Needless to say, Safiyya had not been a slave woman prior to her being treated as lawful plunder. The learned Pakistani translator of *Sahih Muslim* is not satisfied even with this elucidation. Not to be outdone by the venerable Imam of aforetime, he has added his own encomium on the Prophet's noble character on the strength of this very *hadīs*. He speaks of a Revelation (without actually citing it) that "her marriage with the Holy Prophet was a dire necessity in the larger interest of the Islamic State"!! Nor does he stop even at that. He adds in so many words that "It is easy to talk of noble things and high ideals, but it is difficult to put them into practice."!!! Obviously, he enters the event in the register of the Prophet's noblest deeds. Comment is superfluous.[7]

[7] Margoliouth says that the Arabic word 'Safiyya' means 'titbit' i.e. an article specially selected by the conqueror out of the booty. He denies that Safiyya had been her real name. Comment again is superfluous.

9

Jihād in the Shariat

In Islam, the term 'Shariat' is often used to mean the system of ordinances as given in the Koran and the Hadis. But I shall use it in a more restrictive sense—for those ordinances which were formulated in the schools of jurisprudence (*Fiqh*) of the famous Imams Hanīfah, Hanbal, Mālik and Shāfi'ī. The school of Hanīfah being the most popular in the Islamic world, I shall confine my attention to that school alone and use Shykh Burhanuddin Ali's (d. 1198 AD) *Hidāyah* in order to set forth the opinions of the Shariat on the subject of *jihād*.

From the foregoing chapters it would appear that the Koran and the Hadis, between them, have exhausted the subject of *jihād* and that there is little to add to their ordinances. But in fact it is not so. For example, if *jihād* be a Mussalman's supreme duty as indicated in the Koran and the Hadis, a question is inevitable: Is it not proper for a Muslim to be engaged in *jihād* continuously and permanently? Should he not set out on his own to "make slaughter" amongst the infidels without caring for what his fellow Muslims are doing? Not so, says the Shariat; one can engage in *jihād* only when the Imam gives a call for it. In the Prophet's time, he himself was the Imam par excellence. But after him the duty has vested in lawfully constituted Imams. *Jihād* is indeed compulsory for all able-bodied Muslims; it is *farz*—the Arabic word for duty that is binding and unavoidable under all circumstances. But it is not a *farz-i-ain*—the canonical duty binding on every Muslim without reference to any other person. It is a *farz-i-kifāyya*—a duty that can be left to others until the

Imam gives out his call. When the Imam does so it becomes *farz-i-ain* and no able-bodied Mussalman under his jurisdiction can shirk the duty of waging *jihād*. But till that moment he can rest on his oars. Such is the prescription of the Shariat regarding the nature of the duty of *jihād*.

Can any and every Imam of any and every mosque give out the call for *jihād*? The question does not arise in Islamic states where the Sultans and Padishahs count as lawfully constituted Imams. But in non-Islamic states, the question becomes important. Any Muslim leader, even the leader of the congregation for Friday prayers, in non-Islamic countries can put forth his claim for authorising a *jihād*. The Shariat has indeed prescribed certain qualifications for Imamhood, but has not provided any foolproof method for testing such qualifications.

(2) The Shariat has clarified another point which is not mentioned in the Koran or the Hadis with sufficient clarity. Is it necessary to serve a notice to the infidels who are being attacked? The Koran is silent on the question. The Hadis, in the context of the Jews mentioned in a previous chapter, says that the Prophet did serve such notice on at least one occasion. But most of his *jihāds* being in the nature of raids embarked upon in extreme secrecy, these were not usually preceded by formal declarations of war. The Shariat accepts both the provisions, but sets out to explain the importance of prior notification with some care. According to the *Hidāyah*, "[the infidels have to] perceive that they are attacked for the sake of religion, and not for the sake of taking their property, or making slaves of their children".[1] Thus the *Hidāyah* makes the notification compulsory when attacking those infidels who have never been "called to the faith", but makes it optional in other cases.

(3) On the other hand, the Shariat asks the Imam to declare *jihād*, if necessary, by violating or terminating the pacts and treaties previously entered into with the infidels. In other words,

---

[1] *The Hedaya*, translated by Hamilton, Book IX, Chapter II.

the Shariat asks the Muslims to look upon treaties with infidels as no more than temporary expedients to be dispensed with when these no longer serve their purpose. As already mentioned, immunity from such obligation to the unbelievers is enjoined in the Koran itself, but the Shariat spells it out with absolute frankness. Says the *Hidāyah:* "If the Imam makes peace with aliens for a single term, and afterwards perceives that it is most advantageous for Muslims to break it, he may in that case lawfully break it after giving due notice; because upon the change of circumstances ... the breach of peace is war and the observance of it is a desertion of war; and war is an ordinance of God, and the forsaking of it is not becoming."

(4) Is there any room for civilised rules in the war what that is *jihād* ? None whatsoever, declares the Shariat "The Mussalmans must attack the infidels with all manner of warlike engines (as the Prophet did by the people of Taif) and must also set fire to their habitations (in the same manner the Prophet fired the Baweera) and must inundate them with water, and tear up their plantations and tread down their grain. These means are all sanctioned by law."

(5) Is it permissible to kill women and children in *jihād* ? Better not, says the *Hidāyah,* not because they are to be pitied but because they constitute booty. But if the *mujāhid* does kill them, he is not liable to punishment or fine, "because that which protects (that is Islam) does not exist in them". Clearly, the Shariat is no believer in understatement or the soft option.

(6) It is evident that the Shariat is bent upon taking the injunctions of the Koran and the Hadis to their logical end. Thus it is not prepared to release captives even after they have decided to profess Islam. They have to be sold as slaves, says the *Hidāyah* "because the reason for making them slaves had existence previous to their embracing the faith".

(7) Even a non-Muslim captive is not to be ransomed for his Mussalman opposite number. "The argument of Hanifa," says the *Hidāyah,* "is that such an exchange is an assistance to the

infidels; because these captives will again return to fight the Mussalmans which is an evil."[2] In fact, the emphasis in the Shariat is towards slaughtering the kafir prisoners—kafir-slaughter being preferable to having Muslim prisoners released.

It is not possible in so short a notice to do justice to the vast literature of the Shariat on the single subject of *jihād*. But the foregoing material is quite adequate to explain the tendency of this literature. That tendency is to close whatever loophole for charity might exist in the exceedingly sanguinary business called *jihād*. It is not as if the injunctions of the Koran and the Hadis are not sanguinary enough. But the Shariat is all the more so and even a cursory glance at this literature brings out the hollowness of the claim put forth by modern apologists like Maulana Abul Kalam Azad who would have us believe that *jihād* is nothing but a species of defensive warfare. Azad has indeed appealed from the Shariat to the Koran. But as has been clearly pointed out in the previous pages, that book itself suggests very little foundation for such a belief. I have also shown that the Hadis does even less. And the Shariat clinches the matter beyond any scope for ambiguity or equivocation. As the *Hidāyah*, at the very start of its pedantic exercise on the subject of *jihād* points out: "[*jihād*] is established as a divine ordinance by the word of God, who has said in the Koran 'slay the infidels' and also by a saying of the Prophet: 'war is permanently established until the day of the Judgment'." This shows that the Shariat merely confirms the doctrines of the Koran and the Hadis, and adds to them only incidentally.

---

[2] It is, however, fair to mention that the school of Imam Hanīfah is not unanimous on this point.

10

Jihād and Religious Riot

An important question relating to the subject of *jihād* is this: in mixed populations consisting of Muslims and non-Muslims alike, should this sanguinary creed not inevitably lead to religious riots? Certainly, the Koran furnishes us with verses which have the appearance of extremely provocative utterances aimed at rousing the Mussalmans to a state of murderous mob-fury. "Go forth light armed and heavy armed and strive with your wealth and your lives in the way of Allah," says the Koran (9/41). A verse of this kind does look like being more in the nature of a rabble-rousing ejaculation than a proclamation of pre-planned and premeditated warfare. "Slay the idolaters wherever you find them" (9/5) is again, to all appearances, a call to lawless violence rather than a general's directive to draw the battle lines with discipline and forethought. Indeed, the whole group of the so-called Immunity Verses (9/1-12) of the Koran seems for all practical purposes to indicate a sort of abdication of the Islamic state's responsibility for law and order by asking the Muslim masses to destroy the infidel population by whatever means available to them. A close examination of the context and consequences of the verses is, therefore, necessary to investigate the question of the relation of the doctrine of *jihād* to religious riot.

As has been mentioned earlier, the Immunity Verses of *Sūrah Taubah* were issued in early 631 AD to inform the idolaters of Arabia that after the expiry of 4 months their religion would no longer be tolerated. As Mohammed Pickthall, the orthodox translator of the Koran, mentions in the introduction to this *sūrah,* these verses formed the "proclamation of Immunity from obligation toward the idolaters" and "signified the end of idolatry in Arabia". But how was that end to be achieved? By "slaying the idolaters" indiscriminately, says the Koran; by "besieging them" and by "laying for each of them an ambush". In other words, Allah does appear to have sanctioned, by these verses, religious riots on an unprecedented scale.

But did the Prophet so interpret them? The biographies do not narrate any large-scale riot following upon the issuance of these verses. It has to be remembered that the Prophet survived these injunctions by only about a year, and most of the time he was receiving delegations from the tribes of Arabia offering voluntary submission and voluntary adhesion to his creed. Information regarding forcible conversions during the period is scanty; and apart from the riot-mongering verses of the Koran mentioned above, we are not informed of any specific instance of religious riot actually taking place in pursuance of them. In the technical language of Islam, we should say that the riot-mongering verses did not in fact give rise to a body of Sunnah to illustrate them.

But indeed such Sunnah is not necessary. The Islamic concepts of *Dār-ul-Islam* (territory of Islam) and *Dār-ul-harb* (territory of war), which originated from the jihadic provisions of the Koran and the Hadis, seem to have grown out of this very dilemma. These concepts presuppose the extermination of Arabian idolaters by the power of the state, while in non-Arab Islamic states the practice is to spare the lives of idolaters on payment of the poll-tax. Such an arrangement dispenses with the need for religious riots in Islamic states for the simple reason that the state on its own does the work of conversion or refrains from it according to its own convenience. In these states, the populace is absolved from its duty of "slaying the infidels" indiscriminately.

By the same token, non-Islamic states with a large body of Muslim population must of necessity give rise to religious riots, if the Ulema declare these states to be *Dār-ul-harb*. The Immunity Verses of the Koran must, in the nature of things, come into full play in such states. In this restricted sense at least, *jihād* and religious riot are one.

Who would give the call for such riots? It has been shown in the previous chapter that *jihād* cannot start without the Imam pronouncing a call for it. It has also been pointed out that in Islamic states, the king is the person best qualified to pronounce such a call. But in *Dār-ul-harb* such an Imam is obviously not available. So any person with the requisite Islamic qualifications can give the call for *jihād,* and even the Imam who leads the congregation in Friday prayers can very well undertake the job. Needless to say, such a *jihād* can hardly turn out to be anything but a species of religious riot.

To illustrate such *jihāds,* which should more properly be called *jihād*-riots as distinct from a full-fledged *jihād,* I should give some examples from India's recent history. In such a case, historical examples of lesser Imams must replace the Prophet's Sunnah if only because the Prophet's career antedated the doctrine of *Dār-ul-harb.*

(1) The first considerable religious riot in India under British rule was the so-called Mopla rebellion of 1921 which occurred in Malabar as an offshoot of the Khilafat Movement. The Moplas burst into unprecedented violence against the British, following upon the Khilafat Committee's call for the same addressed to the believing population of Malabar. As it turned out, most of the casualties in this *jihād* were Hindus rather than the British. Hundreds of Hindu women jumped into wells to save their honour, others being ravished and slaughtered with absolute indifference by blood-thirsty *mujāhids.* Hundreds of corpses of Hindu women as well as children were recovered from the wells after the end of the riots. The call for this *jihād* had been pronounced by the Ali Brothers, Hasrat Mohani, and Maulana Abul Kalam Azad. Mahatma Gandhi himself acknowledged these atrocities as part of Islam's holy war. He referred to the *mujāhids*

as "God-fearing Moplas" and said: "They were fighting for what they consider as religion and in a manner which they consider as religious." Needless to say, such manner of fighting for such a cause is the essence of an Islamic *jihād.* It should be mentioned that leaders like Azad gave the call for *jihād* against the British rather than the Hindus, but it is not known how they intended to confine the war against a single class of infidels.

(2) The Great Calcutta Killing of 1946 was again the consequence of a call for *jihād,* which in this case was pronounced by Mohammed Usman, the Mayor of Calcutta at that time. He put the call in black and white and addressed the *mujāhids* as follows:

"It was in this month of Ramzan that open war between Mussalmans and Kafirs started in full swing. It was in this month that we entered victorious into Mecca and wiped out the idolaters. By Allah's will, the All India Muslim League has selected the selfsame month of Ramzan to start its *jihād* for realising Pakistan."[1]

(3) The holocaust in Noakhali in the same year (1946) was likewise intended as a full-fledged *jihād.* The call in this case was pronounced by Gholam Sarwar, a Muslim M.L.A. from those parts. Gholam Sarwar's call was not documented, but the report submitted by Judge Simpson clearly refers to "large-scale conversion of Hindus to Islam by application of force in village after village. In many instances, upon the refusal of the menfolk to embrace Islam, their women were kept confined and converted under duress."[2] All these of course were characteristic of a true *jihād.*

This was not all. As in Calcutta, the Noakhali riots were characterised by the dishonouring of thousands of Hindu women. There were clear indications that these unfortunate women were looked upon as the *mujāhids'* lawful plunder *(ghanīmah).* Baboo

[1] Translated from the Bengali original cited in R.C. Majumdar, *Bāṅglādesher Itihāsa,* Volume IV.

[2] Ibid.

Rajendralal Roy, the President of Noakhali Bar Association, attempted to put up on his own some resistance to this *jihād.* The outcome of this resistance has been described by a contemporary writer: "Rajenbaboo's head was presented to Gholam Sarwar on a platter, and two of his lieutenants received as guerdon both of his young daughters (in their harem)."[3]

(4) The large-scale communal riots taking place in places like Aligarh, Bulandshahar and the like in December 1990, were all the handiwork of worshippers proceeding from mosques at the end of the Friday prayers. Most newspapers reported these riots, but none quoted the call given by the Imams.

(5) Almost all Hindus have in recent years been evicted from the Kashmir Valley as a result of *jihād.* This particular *jihād* has been authorised and financed by Pakistan and other Islamic countries. Clinton's America is the latest addition to the names of countries actively promoting this *jihād.* Of course, America has not called it a *jihād* but declared its support of the *mujāhids* in the name of Human Rights, which means the same.

(6) The large-scale arson of December 1992 occurring in Islamic Bangladesh in the wake of the demolition of the Babri structure at Ayodhya was characterised by gangrapes of thousands of Hindu girls, assaults on Hindu temples, and widespread loot and violence. It had all the marks of a full-fledged *jihād.*

All these examples go to show that riots on many occasions break out in the name of *jihād.* I have mentioned Indian examples alone, but similar examples can no doubt be cited from most countries with a substantial Muslim population. It is a moot point whether such *jihād-riots* satisfy all the scriptural requirements of an unadulterated *Jihad fi Sabilillah (jihād* in the way of Allah). But there is little doubt that *jihād-riots* do take place. If a country with a sizeable Muslim population neglects the possibility of their incidence, it does so at its own peril. In India, for example, the ever-increasing uncertainty in Hindu-Muslim rela-

[3] Benoy Bhushan Ghosh, *Dvijātitattva O Bāṅgāli,* p. 68.

tions can be set down to our long-standing failure in taking a clear stand on the subject of riots inspired by the psychology of *jihād* endemic in the Muslim community. Before taking up this topic, I should give a summary of the discussion spread out in the foregoing chapters.

11

Recapitulation

In summing up the contents of this book one must remember that its aim is the exposition of the theoretical aspects of *jihād*, and as such its subject is Islamic tenets rather than Islamic history. This remark applies with equal force to the brief historical accounts of the Prophet's own *jihāds* which this book mentions. These are intended as accounts of the Prophet's Sunnah or practice which is part and parcel of theoretical Islam as distinct from the Islam of history. The distinction is fundamental if only because not everything in the Prophet's own history is considered his Sunnah. His bloodless conquest of Mecca, for example, does not constitute a body of Sunnah, whereas his destruction of the Jewish clan of Kuraizah very much does so. This is because the latter act conforms to the Koranic injunction of "making slaughter in the land" while the former has no such scriptural backing. To put the whole matter in a nutshell: the Koran as the word of Allah supplies the injunction; the Hadis in the language of the Prophet confirms it; and the Sunnah gives a practical demonstration of the same and thereby acts as an exemplar to future performers of the hallowed exercise called *jihād.*

One thing regarding the present discussion requires particular emphasis. The reader must not suppose that my citations from the Koran are by any means full or exhaustive. I have discussed only those verses which seemed relevant to the subject. And as regards the Hadis, my citations have been fewer still. It is not even true that I have selected the most sanguinary verses in order to bring out the true nature of *jihād.* All through, my aim has been to highlight as many aspects of the subject as possible, and for this reason I have not confined my attention to any single aspect, nor overburdened my analysis with innumerable citations. This is why I have not dilated on the speculations of the various schools of Shariat, but referred to only those conclusions which confirm the scriptural injunctions or fix them with greater clarity. On the other hand, as my subject has been primarily Islamic *jihād* as expounded in the canonical literature, I have not referred to the concept of *jihād* as understood by the Sufis, the proponents of Islamic mysticism. But for the sake of completeness, I should mention that, according to some Sufis, the canonical *jihād* is *Jihād al-Asghar* or the *Lesser Jihād* whereas the war against one's sensual proclivities is *Jihād al-Akbar* or the *Greater Jihād.* In a word, the Sufis emphasize self-control rather than war against infidels in their conception of *jihād.* But whatever merit such a conception may possess, it is not known that Sufis in any country under Islam have made the slightest impact on their co-religionists in unsettling the deep-seated convictions regarding the bloodthirsty business that is *jihād.* For this reason, I take note of the Sufi conception of *jihād* for what it is worth, but do not find it necessary to discuss it at length.

If one were to summarise the contents of this book, the point that would need the uttermost emphasis is that *jihād* is a bloody confrontation with unbelievers; it is a war informed by the greatest possible spirit of aggression; and, more often than not, it is a war of deception and subterfuge. "War is stratagem" says the Prophet *(Sahih Muslim,* No.4311)—a *hādis* to which Aurangzeb was particularly addicted. But it would be wrong to suppose that the Koran nowhere mentions *jihād* as a species of war in self-defence. According to verses 2/190-92 of the Koran:

"Fight in the way of Allah against those who fight against you, but begin not hostilities. Lo! Allah loveth not aggressors.

"And slay them wherever ye find them, and drive them out of the places whence they drove you out... And fight them not at the Inviolable Place of Worship until they first attack you there, but if they attack you, then slay them ... But if they desist then lo! Allah is Forgiving Merciful."

These verses clearly preach war in self-defence alone. Although they are sanguinary enough, it is astonishing how they attempt to combine some sort of humanity in a counsel of reckless bloodshed. On the face of it, they do not indeed advocate aggressive warfare, so much so that they forbid excesses committed even in self-defence. But what lurks behind that seemingly benevolent face does not appear all that benevolent. This is a matter on which we need not go by these verses alone. Very many verses of the Koran and the whole of the Hadis literature breathe the spirit of unqualified aggression. We need refer to the Immunity Verses alone (K 9/1-12) to have a feel of that spirit. As regards the Sunnah, not a single *ghazwah* (=war led by the Prophet in person) of the Prophet, barring that of Uhud (AD 625) and Ahzāb (AD 627), can by any stretch of imagination be reckoned defensive war. In other words, 24 out of the 26 *ghazwahs* of the Prophet were aggressive in intent as well as execution. It has been argued that these aggressive confrontations were necessary if only to make Islam survive under uncongenial surroundings. This is at best dubious reasoning if we remember that, at Medina, Islam had found a haven of safety and security. But even if we accept this reasoning as valid, the aggressive nature of the *ghazwahs* of the Prophet can hardly be wished away. What, however, is more to the purpose is the fact that whatever justification we can plead in favour of these wars of early Islam, their status as a body of canonical Sunnah, to be emulated till the end of the world, can hardly be dismissed as a relic of the past. The Koran itself does not always conceal the world-conquering mission of Islam behind ambiguous verbiage. "O ye who believe! What aileth you when it is said unto you: Go forth in the way of Allah, ye are bowed to the ground with heaviness? .. If ye go not forth He will afflict you with a painful doom, and will choose instead of you a folk other than you" (K 9/38, 39). It is this strain which is the informing note of most of the *jihād* verses of the Koran, the verses of self-defence being only a streak of pacifism that is both specious and unconvincing.

(2) A second point of importance arising out of the present discussion is this: the aim and the fruits of *jihād* have all been spelled out in a manner which is in perfect consonance with its overwhelmingly aggressive design and intent. This is why although the conversion of unbelievers to Islam is recognised as the supreme aim of *jihād,* the call for such conversion has not been made a compulsory pre-requisite for mounting a jihadic offensive. This again is the reason why this supreme aim has, in the Koran as well as the Hadis, generally been made subservient to the comparatively minor aims of plunder, *jizyah,* and slaughter. "Eat ye the spoils of war. They are lawful and pure" (K 8/69)—such pronouncements have often been made in a louder and loftier voice than the call for spreading Islam. A *hādis* in the collection by Tirmizī contains the singular exhortation: "Spread ye *salām* (the Islamic mode of salutation); feed ye the people that go without food; and strike ye down the heads of unbelievers." Tirmizī himself considers this *hadīs* as *gharīb,* that is to say, poor in authenticity. But it can hardly be denied that the keynote of the jihadic injunctions of the Koran and the Hadis is the assumption of the most intimate relationship between such expressions of Islamic deportment as *salām* and such Islamic achievements as striking down the heads of unbelievers. It must also be remembered that even the recommendation for concubinage with captured kafir women does not occur in the Koran in only one verse and in an involuntary fit of divinely inspired lasciviousness, so to say. Its repetition in so many verses cannot but raise in our mind the question: could not the repetition of such pronouncements be avoided in what is supposed to be the Holy Book of Islam? Small wonder that religious riots are invariably marked by violation of infidel women, even when loss of life is minimal.

12

Conclusion

In concluding this small treatise on the important Islamic doctrine of *jihād,* the reader must be reminded that it does not purport to be a critique of Islam as such. Even in the restricted field of its survey, its aim has been descriptive rather than critical. But before one leaves the subject it is only fair to address to the reader certain reflections which the foregoing discussion inevitably raises.

(1) The first reflection is on the failure of the world at large to take note of this creed of hate and violence, and get forewarned as to the peril it entails to the civilisation of all non-Muslim peoples including those who profess Christianity. The decline of the West, of which Spengler wrote, is nowhere so evident as in its total indifference to the Islamic doctrine of *jihād,* and in the absolute neglect of its duty to confront such a creed intellectually while broadcasting over the whole world its pernicious implications. Thanks to the money-power of the oilrich Arab countries, Islam has spread its tentacles to the farthest point of the globe, and is making known its intention of world-domination in no uncertain terms. The intellect of the West looks at the spectacle, benumbed and fascinated, sometimes breaking into loud acclamations as to the glory that is Islam, and sometimes mumbling incoherent protests against its 'fundamentalism'. As Nirad Chaudhury has pointed out, this division of Islam into two variants—the one Fundamentalist and the other Liberal—is the result of "either ignorance or repulsive hypocrisy". Whatever else may get liberalised, *jihād*

cannot; and the West's failure to understand the true nature of the current Islamic Revival must be recognised as the most colossal intellectual failure of the present epoch. It is against the background of this failure that a great many contemporary events have to be judged: the West's prevarication with the events in Bosnia or in Kashmir; its impatience with Israel in its life-and-death struggle in surroundings where a single false step could spell its destruction; and, coming to a lower plane, the Prince of Wales's breaking out into singing the glory of Islam from a public platform.

(2) As regards Christian missionaries, their record is worse still. Despite the far flung apparatus of proselytisation they have built up over the centuries, their latter-day flirtation with Islam is probably the stupidest thing these worthies have done at the end of nearly two thousand years of unceasing effort towards leading the 'benighted heathens' of the world to the fold of Christianity. Apparently this flirtation is aimed at peaceful conversion of the pagan peoples of Asia and Africa in some sort of collaboration with the Islamic zealots active in those countries and without causing them any unnecessary heartburn. But it is certainly the strangest marriage of convenience that could ever take place between two parties who have always been at loggerheads with each other. Also it must be remembered that the study of Islam and world's acquaintance with its awful doctrines started with these missionaries themselves. True, after the initial centuries of mud-slinging at the prophet of Islam, Christian scholars had been sobered by the reflection that in view of the identity of their own creed of monotheism with Islam, a wholesale condemnation of the latter would involve a condemnation of their own religion. But till the end of the 19th century these scholars had a clear understanding of their task. They did not fail to recognise the doctrine of *jihād* for what it was—a code of murder and rapine disguised under a thin coating of religious verbiage. Also, however enamoured they might have been of the Koran's full-throated pagan-bashing, they

never forgot the supposed superiority of the Christian revelation. Even so serious a scholar as Sir William Muir did not fail to administer a large dose of Christianity in his monumental biography of the Prophet. Muir knew, as all Christian missionaries knew in those days, that their greatest adversary in the business of proselytisation was Islam. It is therefore incomprehensible that their latter-day descendants should join hands with Islam in every country of Asia and Africa in the game of proselytising the pagans of those lands.

The worth of the short-lived gains they have thus achieved in those countries must be viewed against the forces they have unleashed in their continuing flirtation with the Islamic establishment. They must know that a newly baptized pagan is more vulnerable to the blandishments of Islam than an unregenerate pagan rooted in unalloyed heatheism. The small dose of monotheism administered through Christianity merely removes the pagan's safeguards and renders him inclined to a larger and a more massive dose of the same. And the toothless Christianity of the 20th century, preached by means of fraud and bribery and a prodigious establishment of social service, will certainly prove no match for Islam when the latter sets out to declare full-fledged *jihād* against the converts which Christianity has gained by years of hard labour and a mind-boggling expenditure of money. The Western powers will certainly go through the motions of protesting against the iniquities of such rampant 'fundamentalism', but will do precious little to save those converts for Christianity. Christian missionaries should take lesson from the fate of the Christians under the Ottoman Empire, and, for the matter of that, under its Kemalist successors. Slowly and surely, Turkey has been denuded of the Christian element in its population, with the Western powers looking on in blissful unconcern. There is no reason to believe that the same fate does not await the new converts to Christianity in Asia and Africa. Certainly the present-day flirtation of Christian missionaries with Islam in these countries bodes little good to Christianity's long-term ends. Before it is too late the Christian churches should take a hard look at this self-defeating policy of their missionary establishments and warn their countries as to its possible outcome.

(3) Coming to India, the future of Hindus who form the bulk of the population of this country seems grim indeed if their obstinate refusal to face the reality of the current Islamic Revival with its pronounced jihadic overtones continues as before. Hindus have been victims of *jihād*-riots in an ever-increasing progression since the infamous Mopla riots of 1921. Political independence, besides giving rise to an Islamic state wedded to the goal of reconquering the whole of India for Islam, witnessed a genocidal slaughter of Hindus the like of which is not known in world history. The Indian State since 1947 has persistently refused to investigate these riots and lay bare the jihadic motivation behind them. This, however, is a large subject with prodigious political dimensions, and no proper discussion of it can be made within the compass of this book. I would confine myself to a few remarks of a general nature regarding how Hindus and peace-loving Muslims should address themselves to the Islamic creed under discussion.

As for Hindus, they should clearly understand that the doctrine of *jihād* is absolutely fatal to their life and property, not to speak of the honour of their womenfolk. If the Hindu does not make a serious and determined effort towards persuading his Muslim brethren to renounce the doctrine of *jihād,* if he does not devote his heart and soul to devise adequate means of achieving that end, in a word, if he does not shed his deep-seated indifference to things Islamic, then he is most certainly proceeding towards self-destruction and that too in a not very distant future. To realise the overwhelming urgency of this matter, it is only necessary to point out that, starting from the Islamic revolution of Khomeini's Iran, Muslims all over the world are hell-bent on reviving the jihadic frenzy of 7th century Islam. That Mussalmans of India should continue to feed on such frenzy and that Hindus should persist in their delusion regarding the feasibility of peaceful coexistence with such a frenzied folk, does no longer make sense.

Muslims on their part must clearly understand that the doctrine of *jihād,* however useful it may be in promoting their worldly interests and ensuring their eternal felicity in the hereafter, can hardly command the approbation of men possessed of even a modicum of rationality and sense of justice. An argumentative Muslim might plead *that jihād* is his only weapon for self-defence in a hostile world; but no one in his senses would really declare permanent war against unbelievers on such a plea. Self-defence is certainly every man's birthright and one can very well sympathize with a person going to war in order to establish his birthright; but *jihād* is hardly ever such a defensive war. *Jihād* is total war aimed at exterminating all unbelievers from the face of the earth, and whoever justifies such war on the plea of self defence plays a gigantic game of deception on people's credulity.

If this reasoning be admitted, the question that immediately suggests itself is this: is it possible to have a version of Islam that may be called *Islam without jihād?* Is such an Islam not a truncated Islam? I should attempt an answer to this second question first.

It requires but little reflection to note that Islam in its pure form—the Islam that is firmly and unalterably rooted in the teachings of the Koran and the Hadis—exists nowhere in the modern world. A big example of the altered state of affairs is the obsolescence of slavery and the maintaining of slave concubines which, according to the Koran, is the birthright of every Muslim and the privilege of every *mujāhid.* The practice is sanctioned in the Koran and the Hadis and confirmed by the Prophet's Sunnah. Despite such incontrovertible pleas of legality and respectability, these two customs are no longer defended in Islamic countries, and even the Ulema do not preach these usages with their accustomed fervour. If, however, the Prophet's Sunnah be binding on every Muslim, then it follows that no practice sanctioned by him can count as being of temporary validity. "It becometh not a believing man or a believing woman, when Allah and His Messenger have decided an affair (for them) that they should claim any say (in it)," says the Koran (33/36). If this be true, then it is obvious that the observance of one part of the Sunnah of the Prophet to the neglect of another would prove destructive to the whole theory of the Sunnah. If the Sunnah for the slave concubine be temporary, on what authority will the Sunnah for *jihād* count as permanent? The Koranic authority for both being similar, how do we distinguish between the relative worth of either?

Indeed, the matter does not seem to admit of any very considerable controversy. Theologians of Islam divide the whole gamut of Islamic duties into five clear divisions: (1) *Itiqādāt,* implying matters of belief; (2) *Ādāb,* the system of Islamic moralities; (3) *Ibādāt,* involving matters of religious practice like prayers and fasting including the practice *of jihād;* (4) *Mu'malāt* which includes laws of business transactions; and (5) *Uqūbāt,* penal provisions of Islam. Out of these five divisions, the last two, namely, *Mu'malāt* and *Uqūbāt* are in a state of obsolescence in most countries under Islam. It stands to reason that Islam in its pristine purity is non-existent in most Islamic countries. In view of this it is sheer perverseness to argue that Islamic *Ibādāt* is not susceptible to any such modification as the renunciation of *jihād* would imply.

It may be objected that the Koran pronounces the undertaking of *jihād* to constitute a Mussalman's supreme duty, whereas no such pronouncement is available for divisions like *Mu'malāt* and *Uqūbāt.* But contrariwise, one can also argue that the Sunnah of the Prophet has been declared to be perfect in its totality, the greatest good of a Mussalman's existence being supposed to consist in an unquestioning copying of the Prophet's life-style. Now if the Mussalman, even with such deep-seated conviction regarding the inviolability of Sunnah, can choose to violate the Prophet's Sunnah with respect to slavery and slave concubinage, and indeed to consider such violation as being of perfect validity, then the violation of the injunction of *jihād* can certainly not be faulted on any count. What we should take up instead is an investigation into the obstacles to such a step.

The greatest obstacle is no doubt the education imparted in the *maktabs* and *madrasahs*—the seminaries that teach the tenets of Islam. The Ulema would not allow the infringement of a single tenet, at least on the plane of theory. That they have not renounced even the injunction regarding slave concubines "whom one's right hands possesses", comes out most clearly in communal riots in India in which the violation of Hindu women always forms a part of the ritual. It is doubtful if all communal riots are started by the Ulema, but the lesson that infidel women are lawful plunder for Muslim rioters in their role of *mujāhids* is undoubtedly inculcated in Islamic seminaries managed and governed by the Ulema. Without a thorough-going reform of this system of education, the prospect for *Islam without jihād* is bleak indeed.

It is here that India's Secularism is attended with the biggest question mark in its day to day observance. Since 1947, thousands of Islamic seminaries have sprung up throughout the length and breadth of this country in pursuance of clauses in our Constitution, and the Indian State is prevented from interfering in their management by the operation of those very clauses. Leading the Mussalmans to the path of peaceful coexistence with their Hindu neighbours by appealing to such Secularism, is an expectation ludicrous in itself; but the deception played upon peace-loving Muslims by this sop of Secularism is worse still. The intolerably farcical element in this sordid business is the unceasing propaganda, daily mounted in our media with screaming headlines and loud protestations, in favour of this very Secularism and the State's proclamation that without this policy no communal amity is possible in India. This assertion is of course the exact opposite of the truth. A Secularism that allows reckless proliferation of Islamic seminaries without any attempt to reform their system of education is the surest pathway to unhindered communal discord.

Is it possible to remove these forbidding obstacles? Could those Mussalmans to whom the cause of communal concord is dearer than jihadic outbursts of Islam, devise a way to preach the message of *Islam without jihād?* To outward seeming the feasibility of such preaching appears remote indeed. But even in Islam there are some pathways for peace and communal concord. These are of course narrow and beset with insurmountable hurdles, but honest and sincere endeavour on the part of earnest Mussalmans can perhaps make them broader and more accessible to the generality of Muslims.

It must be remembered that the Koran itself has recorded the hesitant murmurings of certain followers of early Islam who had wanted 'respite' from the duty of *jihād* (4/77), and others who had preferred service to pilgrims as a better Islamic duty than going into battle against infidels (9/19-22). It is true that on both occasion Allah dismissed their conscientious objections peremptorily; but even after that the trend persisted. The *hadīs* which declares that the Prophet had not been sent to preach the pacifism of Jews and Christians acquires significance in this context. The peace-loving Mussalman in our own day can appeal to these incidents and forestall the objection of die-hard *mujāhids* by pleading that Allah himself had enjoined the duty of war as a contingent one necessitated by circumstances.

Indeed a close study of the Koran would convince any one that the duty of *jihād* was all along 'contingent' as distinguished from the 'permanent' duties of prayer, pilgrimage and the like. It was in fact no part of the Meccan dispensation, but was enjoined only in Medina for the expansion of Islam which was made possible only under certain exceptional circumstances. Peace-loving Mussalmans of our time can very well plead that an essentially contingent injunction can claim no permanent validity and that the duty of *jihād* can be set aside following the change of circumstances.

Such a movement for *Islam without jihād* would obviously require a thorough-going reform in the existing scheme of Islamic education obtaining in India. The Indian State's supine indifference to such reform is not only reprehensible in itself, but also goes against all the lessons of history. As early as 1871, W.W. Hunter (in his *Indian Mussalmans)* had impressed upon the then British-Indian Government the absurdity of the British-managed Calcutta Madrassa providing an educational fare in which *jihād* formed a large part of the curriculum prepared for Muslim students. The present Indian State has produced few administrators of Hunter's calibre, and the frequent outpourings of its spokesmen regarding the noble and peace-living faith of Islam are not known to have made the slightest dent into the scheme of Islamic education obtaining under the present regime. Such a scheme of education must be overhauled, yielding place to a more suitable one.

Indeed the movement for *Islam without jihād* can never be organised by Muslims alone, however well-intentioned. Such a movement requires the active cooperation of Hindus as well as the Indian State. Had the Indian State sponsored *Islam without jihād* since its inception, there is little doubt that by now the leadership of the Muslim community would have passed on to peace-loving Muslims. But right from the start the Muslim element in India's political set up had been under the shadow of the Ulema of Maulana Abul Kalam Azad's vintage. Till now the preponderating force in India's polity has been the Azad-Nehru axis. This force never emphasized the possible role of pacifism in Islam. Since the days of the Khilafat agitation, Azad had been proclaiming the role of the sword in Islam. In his view of course this sword was the sword of self-defence, but as has been shown in the course of this work, it is pre-eminently the sword for the destruction of infidels. The confusion was worse confounded by the fathers of our Constitution labouring under an invincible ignorance regarding the tenets of Islam.

If the truth were to be told, the greatest enemies of Muslim pacifism have not been the Ulema but the so-called secularists of India, most of them hailing from Hindu society itself. The ignorance of these worthies in regard to everything Islamic has to be seen to be believed. The only consolation they can derive is from the fact that at present such ignorance is a universal phenomenon. The Western world's intellectual decline is nowhere so manifest as in this context. India's Secularism is on its own admission merely a pale imitation of its Western original which itself has nowhere taken note of the Islamic doctrine of *jihād.* Consequently, the riot-prone behaviour pattern of the immigrant Muslim population in Western countries has left them helpless and guessing. The Western media call it 'ethnic unrest' —a stupid description betraying abysmal ignorance about the nature of Islam.

The Indian State can seek consolation from the fact that its own Muslim problem has gradually tended to become a problem for the whole world. The problem cannot be solved without attempting far-reaching reform in Islam in general and Islamic education in particular. Islam being a world phenomenon, Indians cannot do much towards achieving such reform. But the 'Secular State' of India has never attempted even the little that it could achieve. The State which offers no helping hand to such unfortunate victims of Islam as the helpless Shah Bano and the scholarly Mushir-ul-Hassan but which confers honours on such exponents of *jihād* as Maulana Abul Kalam Azad, has certainly forfeited every right to exist except on the sufferance of the hundreds and thousands of *mujāhids* it sustains and nurtures and daily inspires with the holy resolve to destroy its very foundation.

Appendix I

Jihād and Expulsion of Non-Muslims from Islamic Countries

Is expulsion of non-Muslims from countries conquered by Islam a tenet of *jihād?* The question is important, for a whole chapter of the Koran is concerned with this very topic. *Sūrah* 59 of the Koran is entitled *Hashr* which in plain English means 'banishment'. The *sūrah* refers to the expulsion of the Jewish tribe of Banu Nazir from Medina in early 625 AD. As mentioned earlier, the Jewish tribes of Medina were the first victims of early Islam's plundering expeditions. Banu Kainuka was despoiled and banished in 624 AD. The next year (625 AD) saw the banishment of Banu Nazir. Banu Kuraizah was exterminated in 627 AD. These acts of spoliation and mass-slaughter are celebrated in the Hadis literature with unbounded pride and exultation.

Sahih Muslim devotes a whole chapter to this topic. According to this work, "The Jews of Banu Nadir and Banu Quraiza fought against the Messenger of Allah who expelled Banu Nadir and allowed the Quraiza to stay on and granted favour to them until they too fought against him. Then he killed their men and distributed their women, children and properties among the Muslims. The Messenger of Allah turned out all the Jews of Medina—Banu Qainuqa and the Jews of Banu Haritha and every other Jew who was in Medina." (No. 4364).

The same work cites another *hadīs* according to which the Prophet is supposed to have declared, "I will expel the Jews and Christians from the Arabian Peninsula and will not leave any but

Muslims" (No. 4366).

This practice of expelling non-Muslims gets added confirmation from the example of Umar, the second Caliph, who expelled the non-Medinese Jewish tribes of Khaibar on the strength of this very *hadīs*. The reader would remember that this tribe had been conquered in 628 AD, and the Prophet had spared their lives and habitations by compelling them to pay *jizyah:* Their subsequent expulsion during the rule of Umar is thus narrated by Gibbon: "Under the reign of Omar, the Jews of Chaibar were transplanted to Syria and the caliph alleged the injunction of his dying master, that one and the true religion should be professed in his native land of Arabia."[1]

It would thus seem that expulsion of non-Muslims from lands conquered by *jihād* is sanctioned by both the Koran and the Sunnah. But I have not included this activity as an ingredient of *jihād,* as the Prophet never expelled idolaters from Arabia, nor does the Koran sanction this practice except as an act of retribution. "Drive them out of the places whence they drove you out," says the Koran (2/191), and Muslims over the centuries have not been slow to point out, on the strength of this very verse, that *jihād* does not mean aggression. This of course is nonsense, as I have endeavoured to show by analysing very many passages of the Koran that preach aggression with a vengeance. But the point of the above passage is simply this—the Koran does not expressly sanction expulsion of the generality of non-Muslims from Islamic countries except in special circumstances, and even Jews and Christians outside the limits of Arabia are absolved from any general ban. Also, the scriptural practice of *jizyah* would lose all meaning if any such general ban was ever intended.

Nevertheless, the practice of expelling non-Muslims, sporadically if not systematically, has all along been a time-

[1] Gibbon on Islam is not always a trustworthy chronicler. But the expulsion of the Jews of Khaibar, is attested by all historian of early Islam.

honoured practice in all Islamic countries. Such expulsion should more properly be called 'squeezing out', as Muslims, wherever they reside in large numbers, are prone to squeeze out their non-Muslim neighbours by the sheer pressure of their numbers. Even such an arch-secularist as Mutafa Kemal started his secularist career only after a wholesale expulsion of the Greek population of Turkey. In fairness to Kemal, he did admit a proportionate number of Turks from mainland Greece. But no such plea can be held up in the case of the other Christian population of Turkey, which has gone on being squeezed out from the secularist regime over all these years, slowly but inexorably.

Coming to the Indian 'subcontinent', Hindus started being squeezed out, right from 1947, from the erstwhile East Pakistan, now going by the name of Bangladesh. The process started simultaneously with the holocaust in Punjab where hundreds of thousands of Sikhs as well as mainstream Hindus were butchered in one clean sweep by the marauding *mujāhids* of the newly created state of Pakistan. It has been suggested that Bengali Muslims being of a gentler stock were incapable of such mass slaughter. This may be true to a certain extent, but the exodus of Hindus from East Bengal, sometimes in trickles and sometimes assuming the proportions of a flood, has been a spectacle no less heart-rending in the interminableness of its duration than the wholesale and instantaneous butchery of Punjab. In truth, it has been a tragedy of greater dimensions, showing at once the utter helplessness of the Bengali Hindus in their passive acceptance of their fate and the heartless unconcern of the Hindu-dominated secular state of India. Between them, these helpless Bengali Hindus and the callous Indian State have crowded out the basic feature of this long-drawn-out exodus. That the gentler Bengali Muslims, while flinching at outright mass-slaughter, have never shrunk from their jihadic practice of continuous plunder of Hindu property and consistent dishonour of Hindu women, making the said exodus inevitable, is a story which has remained practically unknown to the world at large.

Indeed, the expulsion of non-Muslims from Islamic countries, while not a positive tenet of *jihād,* has always remained an accessory to it. Not being a positive tenet it cannot form a part of any theoretical exposition of the doctrine of *jihād.* But it has been a fact of Islamic history during the fourteen hundred years of Islam's existence, and it is a poor testament to the historians of the world that not one of them has thought fit to chronicle this Islamic phenomenon in a systematic and chronological form, embracing the whole length and breadth of Islamdom.

Appendix II

Jizyah and the *Zimmī*

The imposition of *jizyah* on a vanquished infidel population being one of the five fundamentals of *jihād,* besides forcible conversions, mass slaughter and the two kinds of *ghanīmah* (=plunder), a short discussion of this tax on religion is essential for a full understanding of the doctrine of *jihād.* Needless to say, every single aspect of *jihād* is aimed at the ultimate Islamic objective of conquering the whole world for Islam, *but jizyah* has a very special role to play in attaining that objective. It is the only activity connected with *jihād* which may be called 'bloodless'. As such this topic merits the closest attention.

It is astonishing that most Muslim historians of our times are out to dismiss *jizyah* as a nominal tax on non-combatant non-Muslims imposed more as a benevolent gesture than as a punishment for infidelity. The reasoning behind this propaganda seems to run somewhat on the following lines: in an Islamic state it is the Muslim population alone which is burdened with compulsory military duty; the infidels are relieved from that arduous task by making nominal payment of a trumpery sum; ergo, *jizyah* is the ultimate expression of the Islamic state's ultimate benevolence towards its infidel subjects.

The only flaw in this shining piece of reasoning is its utter failure to answer a simple but inescapable question: why should the Islamic state be so hard upon its own people while it showers so much benevolence on the accursed infidels? Muslim historians have never attempted to answer this straightforward question.[1]

In truth, *jizyah* has nothing to do with military duty or exemption from it. On the contrary, it is one of the worst devices thought out by Allah in one of his blacker moods for crushing the unbelievers without actually slaughtering them. As the Koran puts it: "Fight against such of those who have been given the Scripture as believe not in Allah nor the Last Day, and forbid not that which Allah hath forbidden by His Messenger, and follow not the religion of truth, until they pay the tribute readily, being brought low" (9/29).

This verse has already been explained in Chapter One, where it was mentioned that *jizyah,* according to the letter of the Koran, is intended only for Jews and Christians—the so-called People of the Scripture (or the Book). The extension of the tribute to idolaters outside Arabia was a development of later times and is nowhere expressly mentioned in the Koran. But here I must point out that the above verse, if it means anything, certainly does not mean any concern with military duty from which the People of the Scripture were to be exempted. It simply pronounces a dire punishment upon Jews and Christians for not embracing Islam the moment they are called upon to do so. As everybody knows, Jews and Christians do believe in a single God even though they do not call him Allah. Also, they emphatically believe in the Last Day. The verse in question, however, seems to allege that not all of them cherish these beliefs and are to be punished for that very reason. This would seem to imply that the concern here is with atheists born of Jewish and Christian parentage rather than with believing Jews and believing Christians. But when in the same breath the verse finds fault with these putative atheists for failing to forbid what Allah "forbids by His Messenger" and goes on to

---

[1] "The theory of some modem writers that the *jiziya* was only commutation money paid for exemption from military service is not borne out by history, for it was as late as 10th May, 1855 that 'the *jiziya* as a tax on the free exercise of religion was replaced by a tax for exemption from military service' even in European Turkey (Jadunath Sarkar, *History of Aurangzeb*, Chapter 34).

couple them with those who "follow not the religion of truth'', the intention becomes clear enough. The verse actually refers to all monotheists who have not embraced Islam and would not do so willingly. For such people Allah himself pronounces *jizyah* as a punishment, which is a punishment for infidelity and nothing else. This is the plain meaning of the verse.

But this is not all. The verse indeed mentions non-Muslim monotheists specifically, but by its very wording leaves room for including any and every non-Muslim ''who does not follow the religion of truth''. Indeed such an extension is implied by the concluding words of the verse itself. These concluding words emphatically specify the tax as a mark of degradation for the payer, who—as the verse goes on to say in so many words—are to be "brought low" in paying it. Other renderings of the verse include an addition which says that the tax is to be paid "with one's own hands"—implying that *jizyah* can never be sent through a messenger or an intermediary, however exalted the social position of the infidel may be. In other words, the Koran makes little concession to the position of *Kitābīs* (People of the Book, i.e. Jews and Christians) in the Islamic scheme of things. It pronounces degradation on all non-Muslims to the uttermost limit.

The Addition in the Sunnah

Nevertheless the Koran, in explaining *jizyah* as a mark of degradation for non-Muslims, does not exhaust the subject. For one thing, it nowhere mentions the rate of the taxation. Rather, surprisingly, the Hadis literature also does not discuss it with the fullness which it bestows on other topics. *Sahih Muslim,* for example, has only a single *hadīs* concerned with this all-important subject. Beyond mentioning that ''if they refuse to accept Islam, demand from them the *Jizya''* (No. 4294), it seems to avoid the topic altogether. To fill in the gap, we have to examine the biographical *ahādīs* for further information on *jizyah.*

But even these *ahādīs* do not mention any uniform rate of

taxation. As mentioned in the course of this book, the Jews of Khaibar were the first people to be treated as *kharājguzārs,* that is to say, the payers of the poll-tax. But the tax imposed on these people consisted in leaving them as tenants in their own lands—the rate of taxation, according to Sir William Muir, being half the produce of these lands. This rate was not applied to the Christian governor of Aila whom the Prophet vanquished during the course of the Tabuk campaign (630 AD). The Christian subjects of this monarch were called upon to pay a gold piece (*dīnār*) per head per annum. According to D.S. Margoliouth, the Jews of Aila had to pay a higher rate—one-quarter of their produce. Margoliouth contrasts this rate with the rate of *zakāt* (= alms or poor-due) imposed on Muslims and says that "twenty five percent of the produce means ten times the amount imposed on the Muslims as alms''. On this reckoning, the Jews of Khaibar had to pay a poll-tax twenty times the amount of the corresponding *zakāt* money.

Jizyah in the Shariat

The non-uniform rate of taxation imposed by the Prophet on the various non Muslim tribes of Arabia (and beyond) was a source of endless controversy among the jurists of the ensuing ages; the Caliphs, starting with Umar, did not follow the divergent practices of the Prophet but sought to bring in a measure of uniformity in their own practice. The school of jurisprudence according to Imam Hanīfah, enjoined their practice as canonical. Umar divided the infidel population of his empire into three classes—'the rich', 'the middling', and 'the labouring poor'. On the first class he imposed a tax of 48 *dirhems* per head per annum, on the middling that of 24, and on the labouring poor 12 *dirhems*. As the *Hidāyah* puts it, "The common rate is fixed by the Imam imposing upon every avowedly rich person a tax of forty-eight *dirms* per annum or four *dirms* per month; and upon every person in middling circumstances, twenty-four *dirms* per annum or two *dirms* per month; and upon the labouring poor twelve *dirms* per annum or one *dirm* per month.''[2]

It is not clear whether this fixed rate of taxation was intended for all time to come or whether a percentage on the total income was contemplated by the jurists of the school of Hanīfah in their calculation of the rate. Certainly, the Mughal emperor Aurangzeb imposed the same rate upon the Hindus of India in the seventh decade of the seventeenth century. But even with the possible rise of the price index since the first imposition of this rate, the poorest section of the non-Muslim population had to bear the brunt of this 'benevolent' imposition. Jadunath Sarkar in his *History of Aurangzeb* discusses this question at some length and says: ''In violation of the modem canons of taxation, the *jaziya* hit the poorest portion of the population hardest. It could never be less than Rs. $3\frac{1}{3}$ on a man, which was the money for nine maunds of wheat flour at the average market price at the end of the 16th century. The State, therefore, at the lowest incidence of the tax, annually took away from the poor man the full value of one year's food as the price of religious indulgence.'' Such was the 'benevolent' nature *of jizyah* in Aurangzeb's time.

Jizyah as Retribution Money

Incidentally, the *Hidāyah* brings out the true character of *jizyah* with transcendent clarity. "The capitation tax," it declares, "is a species of punishment, inflicted upon infidels on *account of their infidelity, whence it is termed Jizyat, which is derived from Jizya, meaning retribution."* Again, *"Capitation tax is a sort of punishment inflicted upon infidels for their obstinacy in infidelity,"*[3] The author continues this reasoning to its logical end and gives his own gloss on the all-important Koranic verse (9/29). He says in so many words: ''Whence it is that it cannot be accepted of the infidel if he send it by the hands of a messenger, but must be exacted in a mortifying and humiliating manner, by

[2] *The Hedaya,* Book IX, Chapter 8. The author adds: "(This) doctrine is adopted from Omar, Othman and Ali."

[3] Ibid. Emphasis added.

the collector sitting and receiving it from him in a standing posture; (according to one tradition), the collector is to seize him by the throat, and shake him saying 'Pay your tax, Zimmee' ."[4] The *Hidāyah* thus makes short work of the modern Muslim apologist's attempt to hold up *jizyah* as the expression of the Islamic state's ultimate benevolence to infidels.

Indeed, the *Hidāyah* makes no bones about the long-term objective of *jizyah*, which is nothing short of forcing the helpless *kharājguzār* into the fold of Islam. "If a person becomes a Musulman, who is indebted for any arrear of capitation tax, such arrear is remitted. The Prophet has declared that 'capitation tax' is not incumbent upon Musulman. (Hence this) temporal punishment for infidelity is remitted in consequence of the faith." Shaikh Burhanuddin Ali has explained the real intention of *jizyah* with luminous perspicuity.

It is not that the military intention is wholly absent from the minds of the authors of the Shariat. The retribution money extorted from non-Muslims can be put to many an Islamic use, one of which is doubtless the mounting of newer and fresher *jihāds* for bringing over newer and fresher countries under the umbrella of Islam. The *Hidāyah* recognises this "aid to the troops" of Islam as a lawful use of *jizyah*, and rationalises the division of the *kharājguzārs* (= payers of *jizyah*) into the three classes mentioned above by arguing that "capitation tax is due in lieu of assistance (in *jihād*) with person and property; but as property is different with respect to being more or less, so in the same manner is its substitute (i.e. *jizya)* different."[5] This is the only species of exemption from military duty recognised by the Shariat—it is for the replenishment of war-treasury, not for sparing non-Muslims from arduous military duty.

---

[4] Ibid.

[5] Ibid.

The Meaning of *Zimmī*

In Islam, the *kharājguzārs* (= payers of *jizyah)* are termed *zimmīs*. The literal meaning of this Arabic expression is "people under tutelage"—in other words, people whom the Islamic state holds as hostages to earn an adequate amount of retribution money by exploiting them till the end of their days except when the paying of the tribute is terminated by voluntary conversion. The term itself is an insulting one, but the various disabilities imposed on *zimmīs* by the Shariat leave one wondering whether the plain meaning of the term was not a hundred times preferable to the provisions of the Shariat. Before we discuss some of these provisions, a preliminary word is necessary.

The notion of *zimmī* is not Koranic, and even the Hadis mentions it only in passing. Like so many oppressive measures against non-Muslims, this notion in its fullness is credited to Umar who, on the strength of these very measures, has come to occupy a place among Islamic heroes which is second only to that of the Prophet. It was Umar who defined the *zimmī's* place in an Islamic state in a document which has been quoted in full in Volume VI of *The History and Culture of the Indian People* edited by R.C. Majumdar. I shall not discuss this document here, but set forth only some of its provisions in the language of the *Hidāyah*.[6]

(1) In the first place, the distinction between a Muslim and a *zimmī* is one of the basic tenets of the Islamic state. This distinction has to be maintained at all levels not excluding such matters as 'dress or equipage'. According to the *Hidāyah;* "It is not allowable for Zimmees to ride upon horses, or to use armour, or to use the same saddle and wear the same garments or head-dresses as Musulmans. (Also) the Zimmees must be directed to wear (a woolen rope called) Kisteej[7] openly, on the outside of their clothes. They must be directed, if they ride any animal, to

---

[6] See also *Jizyah* by Harsha Narain.

[7] A woollen band.

provide themselves a saddle like (that) of an ass. (This is because) the Musulmans are to be held in honour, contrary to Zimmees who are not to be held in honour. And if there were no outward signs to distinguish Musulmans from Zimmees, these might be treated with the same respect, which is not allowed. (This is why) the insignia incumbent upon them to wear is woollen rope,... and not a silken belt."

(2) The *Hidāyah* mentions many other modes of discrimination. "It is requisite that the wives of Zimmees be kept separate from the wives of Musulmans, both in the public roads and also in the baths. And it is also requisite that a mark be set upon their dwellings, in order that beggars who come to their doors may not pray for them. The learned have also remarked that it is fit that Zimmees be not permitted to ride at all except in cases of absolute necessity. (And if he rides) he must alight wherever he sees any Musulmans assembled."

(3) Can the *zimmī* be allowed to observe his religious practices? Says the *Hidāyah:* "The construction of churches or synagogues in the Musulman territory is unlawful; but if places of worship originally belonging to Jews and Christians be destroyed or fall into decay they are at liberty to repair them... If however... they build them in (a new) situation, the Imam must prevent them."

"It is not necessary to enumerate all the other disabilities incumbent upon a *zimmī* in an Islamic state. These few restrictions are an adequate indication of his status in any country under the umbrella of Islam. It has often been said that *zimmī*s are second class citizens. The forgoing account shows that they are actually non-citizens in a state of degradation worse than that of the beasts of burden.

The Modern Glorification of the Status of *Zimmīs*

It is interesting but hardly surprising to find that Muslim scholars who have held up *jizyah* as the expression of Islam's ultimate benevolence to non-Muslims, have also hailed the status of *zimmī* in the Islamic state as one of much consequence and considerable dignity. One such scholar has even described the curse of zimmihood incumbent on a non-Muslim in an Islamic state as a process of "raising the unbeliever to the dignity of zimmee". Such monstrous idealisation of such a monstrous doctrine inevitably raises the question: does it not indicate Islam's utter loss of self-confidence in preaching the truth about itself to a world which would reject its pretensions the moment that truth comes to be examined in the court of objective and disinterested scholarship?

This is a question the reader must answer for himself. I would only remark that as early as 1916 Jadunath Sarkar had taken note of this newfangled idealisation of *jizyah* and *zimmī* in his monumental work on Aurangzeb, and demolished it with prodigious wealth of historical facts and masterly presentation from which those facts originated. But even he failed to kill the false propaganda regarding the meanings of *jizyah* and *zimmī,* which in our times has become all the more impudent and universal. This would seem to indicate that the proverbial nine lives of the cat are as nothing compared to the life-span of Islam's propaganda gimmick. Such persistent falsification of well-known facts about Islam can be combated only by an equal persistence with the truth regarding those facts. *Jizyah* and zimmihood are two of the monotonous gifts of Islamic statecraft to the annals of human history, and they have to be shown up again and again for what they truly represent, till an unmindful world takes note and makes adequate preparation for preventing any repetition of mischievous misrepresentation.

Appendix III

Development of the Doctrine of *Jihād* in the Koran

The study of any Islamic doctrine as it developed step by step in the Koran is important on many counts. Not least among these is the consideration as to how far the doctrine was moulded by pressure of immediate circumstance, and how far it stood for any perennial religious concern. As regards *jihād* this question can be answered with some assurance. For *jihād* was never contemplated in Mecca where the Koranic verses started being revealed from 609-10 AD onwards and continued upto 622. It was in the Medinese *sūrahs* alone that *jihād* was enjoined right from the beginning, and by the time the 9th *sūrah* was revealed towards the end of the Prophet's career it became the chief concern of Islam overshadowing every other concern. Chronologically these *sūrahs* mark a clear change of tone and temper. What begins as a hesitant call to arms for the defence of 'Mosques, Churches and Synagogues' ends by being transformed into a violent call for all round destruction of non-Muslims, working murder and rapine all along the line.

The reader must remember that although the *sūrahs* revealed at Medina can be broadly arranged in a chronological series, scholars are by no means unanimous as to the chronology of individual verses. All Koranic scholars are agreed that verses revealed on very different occasions are included in a single *sūrah* without any reference to their date of revelation. With this warning, a broad analysis of the jihadic verses can be made so as to bring out the historical development of their message.

Stage 1

The first stage in the pronouncements on *jihād* is marked by a tone of apology and fervent insistence on the necessity for war by representing the Muslims as a sort of a beleaguered garrison whose only assurance of safety lay in taking up arms rather than in peaceful pursuit of their religion. Roughly, this stage extends from 622 AD to early 626 AD. It is interesting to note that plunder, though already recognised as a legitimate aim of *jihad,* is at this stage made subservient to the aim of defeating and slaughtering the infidels (K 8/69). Forcible conversion on any massive scale is not contemplated.

"Sanction is given unto those who fight because they have been wronged; and Allah is indeed able to give them victory; those who have been driven from their homes unjustly only because they said: Our Lord is Allah. For had it not been for Allah's repelling some men by means of others, cloisters and churches and oratories and mosques, wherein the name of Allah is mentioned, would assuredly have been pulled down" (K 22/39-40).

These verses are extremely interesting as calling for *jihād* in a tone of injured innocence. Sir William Muir has placed these among the earliest jihadic verses, and, if the traditional ascription of their being the very earliest be taken into account, they reveal a most interesting psychology. Allah's concern for 'cloisters and churches' turns out to be a cruel joke, when we consider that within a few years the Prophet would start demolishing the idol-temples of Hijāz with joyous abandon, and, after him, Muslim armies would fan out farther afield to destroy the 'churches and cloisters' in hundreds and even thousands in conquered Christian countries. The joke seems all the more atrocious in its concern for the fate of 'mosques' of which at the time of this revelation there were at most two in existence, and they were never subject to the least apprehension of attack. These verses, therefore, foreshadow the stock Islamic argument advanced during the last several centuries against other peoples' places of worship, namely, that their own places of worship were somehow endangered by the former. But the point here is that these earliest verses of *jihād* are apologetic in tone and betray an uncertainty regarding the reaction of its hearers to Allah's sophistical pleading for war. The only grain of truth in this tissue of untruths is that Muslims had to leave Mecca under some sort of duress as the Koreish would not listen to long-drawn-out palavers for the destruction of their own mode of worship.

"Warfare is ordained for you though it is hateful unto you, but it may happen that ye hate a thing which is good for you, and ye love a thing which is bad for you" (K 2/216).

Here again the tone of apology is manifest. Allah all but grants that war is a 'hateful thing', but pleads that even a seemingly hateful thing may be ordained by him under certain circumstances.

"They question thee (O Muhammad) with regard to warfare in the sacred month. Say, Warfare therein is a great (transgression) but to turn (men) from the way of Allah and to disbelieve in Him and in the inviolable place of Worship (i.e. the Kaba) and to expel people thence is greater with Allah, and persecution is worse than killing" (K 2/217).

This verse is another piece of incredible sophistry. Traditionally it refers to the raid at Nakhla (late 623 AD) in which, according to Ibn Ishāq, the first blood for the cause of Islam was shed in the sacred month of Rajab. It is said that the Prophet was at first embarrassed by this spilling of innocent blood by his followers in the season of peace, but Allah showed him a way out by this very verse. Here again, the migration of Muslims from Mecca, which was at least partly voluntary, is made much of, and concern is even shown for being denied participation in the (idolatrous) worship of Ka'bah. Aggression and unprovoked spilling of innocent blood was never covered up more sanctimoniously than in this verse.

Stage 2

The second stage in the development of the doctrine of *jihād* is revealed most clearly in *Sūrah.* 48. The stage extends (roughly) from 627 AD to the conquest of Mecca (630 AD). This stage is mostly concerned with the sanctification of plunder, the lure of which is the keynote of the *Sūrah Fath* (K/48). This *sūrah* has been discussed in extenso previously. The mask of apology has been dropped at this stage but mass conversion and *jizyah* are not yet mentioned.

The Final Stage 3

The final stage is revealed in *Sūrah Taubah* (the 9th *sūrah)* which has already been discussed in detail. This contains the ban on idolatry in Arabia. It pronounces the immunity from truce with idolaters. It institutes *jizyah.* It again calls for destruction of even mosques not sanctioned by the Prophet (K 9/107). Above all, the mask of apology is so far thrown aside that Allah pronounces the imperialist doctrine of conquest for glory in the following words:

"If ye go not forth He will afflict you with a painful doom, and will choose instead of you a folk other than you" (K 9/39).

These stages and the development of the jihadic theory they represent, prove with transcendent clarity (if indeed any proof was needed) that *jihād* was never contemplated as a permanent dispensation by Allah until almost towards the end, when the all round victory of Islam was assured in Arabia. The doctrine developed by stages and by the exigencies of the political situation and was never anything but an ad hoc dispensation. There is thus every reason to suggest that it be renounced as all ad hoc dispensations are renounced when their need ceases, and the lineaments of a peaceful Islam be conjured up and given shape by people who know better and see further.

Appendix IV

Akbar's Attitude to *Jihād*

The story of how Akbar, the Mughal emperor, earned the title of *ghāzī* by beheading the defenceless Himu on November 5, 1556, and its repudiation by his court historians (Abul Fazl etc.) is a silent commentary on the doctrine of *jihād* by the one and the only Muslim potentate of medieval times who had a wiser head on his shoulders. I give below the two versions of the story—one from the pen of the Afghan historian Ahmad Yadgar and the other from that of Badauni (who drew his material from Nizamuddin's *Tabaqāt-i-Akbarī).* I need only add that Nizamuddin, Abul Fazl, and Faizi—all give the same fabricated version of the story.

According to Ahmad Yadgar, "By the decree of the Almighty an arrow struck Himūn in the forehead... (His soldiers) saw how matters stood, and he sustained a complete defeat. When Shāh Kulī Beg was told of what had occurred, he came up to the elephant (of Himūn) and brought it into the presence of Bairam Khān. Bairam Khān... caused Himūn to descend from the elephant and took him before the young and fortunate prince and said, 'As this is our first success, let your Highness's own august hand smite this infidel with the sword.' The Prince, accordingly, struck him and divided his head from his unclean body."[1]

---

[1] Elliott and Dowson, Vol. V, pp. 65-66. *Tārīkh-i-Akbarī* of Muhammad 'Ārif Qandhārī also says that "The King struck Himu with his sword and won the title *of* Ghazi" (English translation by Tanseem Ahmad, Delhi, 1993, p. 74).

It has only to be remarked that modern historians accept this version alone as the true story of how Akbar earned the title of *ghāzī* (= slayer of infidels) after the Second Battle of Panipat. They do not credit the story circulated by court historians like Nizamuddin and Abul Fazl, which in due course was taken up by Abdul Kadir Badauni.

According to Badauni, "(Bairam Khan said): 'This is your first war *(ghazd),* prove your sword on this infidel, for it will be a meritorious deed.' Akbar replied: 'He is now no better than a dead man, how am I to strike him? If he had sense and strength, I would try my sword.' Then in the presence of them all, the Khan as a warrior of the faith, cut him down with the sword."[2]

This version of the story is extremely interesting, and, as an indication of Akbar's mind at its maturity, is far more valuable than the true story itself. The reader of the present work would understand that in *jihād* there is absolutely no room for chivalry to the fallen enemy. In 627 AD the Banu Kuraizah in chains were cut off at the market place of Medina with nauseating cruelty and little consideration for norms of chivalry. The fourteen-year old Akbar, at the bidding of Bairam Khan, had certainly cut off the head of the defenceless Himu in 1556, confirming thereby the classical Islamic practice. But his court historians knew enough of the Emperor's mind at its maturity to realise that this story would never do in a general history of his reign. They 'paltered with the truth' of history, or rather Akbar himself did so, but they did reveal, as if in a flash, the aging emperor's contempt for the doctrine of *jihād* and the glory of ghazihood that went with it.

---

[2] Ibid., p. 253. Akbar's court historians have also suppressed the fact that Akbar had viewed as *jihād* his expedition to Chittor in 1567-68 in which he had ordered the massacre of 30,000 Hindus, including non-combatants. The text of his *Fathnāma,* issued from Muinuddin Chishti's *dargah* at Ajmer in March 1568, was included in *Munshāt-i-Namakīn* compiled in 1598 by Saiyid Abdul Qasim Khan, a prominent noble who served under Akbar as well as Jahangir. The *Fathnāma* cites the jihadic verses from the Koran, and refers to Hindus as accursed infidels. It has been translated into English by Ishtiaq Ahmed Zilli, and published in *Proceedings of the Indian History Congress*, 1972 (pp. 350-61).

But this is not all. Besides his contempt for *jihād,* Badauni's account contains an ideal of chivalry maturing in Akbar's mind which was little different from the Rajput ideal. That ideal again was the Hindu ideal of chivalry par excellence, harking back to the heroic exploits described in the Mahabharata. It has often been remarked that Akbar's brand of religious tolerance was more a matter of policy than conviction; but the above account indicates how, with advancing years, he inclined with his whole heart towards Hindu ideals and abhorred Islamic teachings in the secret recesses of his being. No wonder, Islamists have never forgiven him for such transparent indications of downright apostasy.

Appendix V

Doctrine of *Jihād* as Defensive War

This book has attempted to show by means of adequate citations from the Koran that *jihād* is aggressive war par excellence, with one or two verses thrown in, in between, to indicate that counsels of moderation and non-aggression are not wholly absent from the Islamic scheme of things. But as Islamic apologists the world over have of late started protesting rather loudly that Koranic' *jihād* is war in self-defence and nothing else, it is important that we discuss threadbare the worth of the Koranic verse which is most often referred to in this connection.

The verse in question is K2/190 which in Marmaduk Pickthall's translation professes to enjoin:

"Fight in the way of Allah against those who fight against you, but begin not hostilities, Lo ! Allah loveth not aggressors."

Taken in isolation, this verse has almost a Gandhian ring. But as indicated in Chapter 11, the immediately succeeding verse makes the uncompromising declaration:

"And slay them wherever ye find them, and drive them out of the places whence they drove you out, for persecution is worse than slaughter" (K2/191).

This verse has nothing Gandhian in it—quite the contrary. It breathes a spirit of uncompromising vengeance rendered worse by the commoner versions of the last clause, which in Sir William Muir's, N.J. Dawood's and Yusuf Alie's translation says: "for idolatry is worse than carnage" instead of "for persecution

---

[1] The emphasis is on the qualifying expression 'Koranic'.

is worse than slaughter". If the ultimate justification for such fierce vengeance is the enemy's alleged crime of idolatry, we are driven to conclude that the *non-aggression* counselled in K2/190 is only a cover behind which the ferocity of the *jihād* business is to be cleverly concealed. The ferocity comes out no less clearly in Pickthall's rendering of 2/191 than in the other renderings.

This explanation of the matter receives added confirmation from other versions of K2/190 in which the reference to *non-aggression* is conspicuous by its absence, and the verse turns out to be nothing more than a plea for *compensatory retaliation* (so to speak). Thus in Muir's rendering the verse has this to say:

"Fight in the way of God with them that fight against you: but transgress not, for God loveth not the Transgressors" (K2/190).

In this rendering as also in Pickthall's version, the first sentence enjoins *compensatory retaliation.* The second part merely asks the 'believer' to desist from transgression and nothing else. Now as *transgression of the limits of Allah* is one of the stock phrases of the Koran, the balance of credibility is in favour of Muir's rendering which is totally silent about the non-aggression clause. Pickthall's rendering is suspect on two counts. First, in his rendering the verse 2/190 is completely at variance with the succeeding verse which enjoins terrible vengeance upon the putative peace-loving Mussalman with a Gandhian outlook. In the second place, the fact of the Koran preaching non-aggression is totally out of tune with other verses, notably the Immunity Verses (K9/1-12) and many others of a similar tenor.

As for *compensatory retaliation* the sentence 'fight against those who fight you' does not preclude the possibility of starting the fight on one's own, but merely emphasizes the duty of hitting back when the fighting is started by the enemy. But even the plea for hitting back when attacked has a ring of speciousness in the Koran which comes out clearly when contrasted with such verses as:

"Warfare is ordained for you although it is hateful unto you; but it may happen that ye hate a thing which is good for you and ye love a thing that is bad for you. Allah knoweth, and ye know not (K2/216, Pickthall's translation).

This verse, which preludes the second set of jihadic pronouncements included in the second chapter of the Koran, is disarming in its candour as regards the excellence of jihadic war as an end in itself. Certainly this verse does not preach *compensatory retaliation,*—very far from it. Allah ordains warfare for the believer and there's an end of the matter. The believer can do nothing about it for Allah has foreclosed all avenues of escape.[2]

As if to drive the point home with redoubled emphasis, the immediately succeeding verse (K2/217) sets out to justify unprovoked bloodshed even in the season of peace. All commentators agree that this verse refers to the raid at Nakhla (Late 623 AD) in the sacred month of Rajab against an unarmed caravan of the Meccans. It was in this raid (as the earliest biographer of the Prophet, Ibn Ishāq remarks) that "the first booty was obtained by the Muslims, the first captives seized and the first life taken by them". Far from being an act of *non-aggression* it could not even count as *compensatory retaliation* by any stretch of imagination. If it was intended as compensatory retaliation for the Muslims' supposed expulsion from Mecca in the first place—such in fact is the drift of the reasoning used in this verse—it was the most dastardly act of retaliation possible.[3] As for being an act of non-aggression, such an interpretation is of course absolutely frivolous.

To sum up, the Koran does not even preach the doctrine of *compensatory retaliation* in the sense of adequately hitting back

---

[2] The reader will remember that the Koran often refers to the believer's reluctance to engage in violent confrontations. Allah everywhere holds such reluctance culpable.

[3] Historically, the Migration *(Hijrat)* was not an expulsion but a voluntary withdrawal from Mecca for the purpose of waging war against the Koreish. Thus the reasoning itself is worthless.

at an enemy who was the first to attack. It preach hitting back ten-fold or hundred-fold. As for non-aggression, the whole tenor of the jihadic verses of the Koran is against such an interpretation. The handful of verses with a conciliatory ring, when closely examined, brings out the vengeful and aggressive intent lurking beneath a string of plausible words. The theory of *jihād* as defensive war must, in the circumstances, be rejected as a figment of the modern apologist's imagination. The figment does not bear even the most superficial scrutiny.

Index